# Eyewitness
# Spy

Night-vision
goggles

Handheld
transmitter

Laptop computer
trace showing
presence of bug
in a building

James Bond's
piton gun from
*Goldeneye*

Side view of
explosives pack for
stay-behind agents
in the event of World
War III occurring

Ultraviolet
lantern and
antibugging
seals

Prints made by SOE agent's rubber
soles used to disguise beach landings

Ox-tongue tin can for
smuggling maps and
compasses, World War I

German invisible ink
and sponge

# Eyewitness
# Spy

Written by
RICHARD PLATT

Photographed by
Geoff Dann and Steve Gorton

SOE rubber soles worn
on boots to disguise
landings on beaches
and in deserts

Leather boot heel
with concealed
compartment,
World
War II

Message hidden
in rubber boot
heel, World
War II

DK Publishing

Counter-
espionage
mirror for
looking
around
corners

Transmitter
for bugging
room

# LONDON, NEW YORK,
# MELBOURNE, MUNICH, AND DELHI

**Project editor** Miranda Smith
**Art editor** Kati Poynor
**Assistant editor** Julie Ferris
**Managing editor** Gillian Denton
**Managing art editor** Julia Harris
**Production** Charlotte Traill
**Picture research** Sarah Moule

**REVISED EDITION**
**Editors** Jayne Miller, Steve Setford
**Art editors** Edward Kinsey, Peter Radcliffe
**Managing editor** Camilla Hallinan
**Managing art editor** Owen Peyton Jones
**Art director** Martin Wilson
**Associate publisher** Andrew Macintyre
**Production editor** Laragh Kedwell
**Production controller** Pip Tinsley
**Picture research** Myriam Megharbi

This Eyewitness ® Guide has been conceived by
Dorling Kindersley Limited and Editions Gallimard

First published in the United States in 1995
This revised edition published in 2009 by DK Publishing,
345 Hudson Street, New York, New York, 10014

Copyright © 1995, © 2009 Dorling Kindersley Limited

13 10 9 8 7 6 5 4 3 2
016 – ED772 – Jul/2009

A catalog record for this book is available from the Library of Congress
ISBN 978-0-7566-5034-6 (HC); 978-0-7566-5035-3 (ALB)

Color reproduction by Colourscan, Singapore
Printed and bound in China by South China Printing Co. Ltd

Discover more at
# www.dk.com

Silk map of
France used
by wartime
agent

Handheld
transmitter
or "bug"

Doll made in Fresnes prison, France,
by World War II agent Odette Sansom

Matchbox created for Special
Operations Executive agent

# Contents

Communications satellite
spying from the sky

# What is a spy?

SPYING, ALSO CALLED ESPIONAGE, began thousands of years ago, with nations battling for land, wealth, or slaves. Spies sneaked into the camps of their enemies, counting the number of warriors, or looking for plans of attack. If they were successful they returned as heroes with the intelligence—the secrets— they had uncovered. Those who failed and were caught faced execution. Throughout history, generals, governments, and business people have used words like CONFIDENTIAL and TOP SECRET to guard important data or documents. Spies are employed by such people to find out information that enemies would rather keep hidden, and pass secrets to people who were not originally intended to know them. Today, spies still live dangerous lives. Some work like burglars to collect intelligence. Some have access to secrets because other people trust them. Spies most often reveal their secrets when enticed by money or to support another country's political system.

*Rahab, who marked her windows with a red cord*

*Joshua watches as the walls of Jericho tumble down*

**BIBLE ESPIONAGE**
A story in the Old Testament, the holy book of Judaism and Christianity, tells how spies helped defeat the walled city of Jericho. The leader of the attacking army, Joshua, sent two spies into the town at dusk. They went to the house of a prostitute, Rahab, and hid on the roof. Rahab lied to the Jericho authorities to protect the spies, and when Joshua's troops destroyed the city, they spared the lives of Rahab and her family, but killed everyone else.

**EGYPTIAN SPY**
Ankhesenamen, young queen of Egypt, wanted to remarry when her husband Tutankhamun died in 1327 BCE. She wrote to a neighboring king: "Send me one of your grown-up sons… he shall be king over Egypt." Instead, the king sent his assistant as a spy to check the queen's story.

## ALEXANDER THE GREAT
The Macedonian king Alexander the Great (356–323 BCE) used spies to find out about enemies' troop movements and also to scout the best marching routes for his massive armies. Alexander's spies used a simple but effective technique to keep their messages secret. They wrote on narrow scrolls spiraling around a stick. Unwinding the scroll broke up the words of the message. But, wound around an identical stick, the text was easy to read.

## SPYING FOR THE MONGOLS
Spies helped Genghis Khan (1162–1227) to conquer most of Asia. Khan came from Mongolia in central Asia, but he knew that people from Mongolia would soon arouse suspicion in distant lands. So he shrewdly recruited spies from among the target peoples, and these local spies were able to move around freely collecting intelligence. Over longer distances, he used horsemen who could ride ten times faster than an army could march to carry his secret messages.

Detail from 1459 map by Fra Mauro, showing Cathay, north China—part of Khan's vast empire

*The Bayeux Tapestry is actually embroidery on a linen strip 230 ft (70 m) long*

*Patterned bag hides camera lens*

## UNNOTICED IN THE CROWD
Some of the greatest spies of the past have been female: women could often go unnoticed where a man would arouse suspicion. In wartime, almost all young men joined the armed forces, and a man in civilian clothes was an unusual sight. In this photograph of Dutch spies at work during World War II (1939–1945), one of the women takes a picture with a hidden camera.

Daniel Craig as James Bond

## RECORDED FOR POSTERITY
The Bayeux Tapestry shows spies in the historic Battle of Hastings in England in 1066. The tapestry records how an army from northwest France, led by William of Normandy (1028–1087), conquered England in 1066. English spies reported sighting thousands of clean-shaven men with short hair. At that time in England, all men except priests wore moustaches and long hair, so the spies assumed that they had seen thousands of French priests. In fact, these "priests" were soldiers who greatly outnumbered the English.

## FICTIONAL SPIES
Dashing spy James Bond, agent 007, is the hero of 13 novels by English author Ian Lancaster Fleming (1908–1964) and more than 20 films based on them. Fleming was himself a spy before he began his career as a writer. He used the people he met during that time as models for the characters in his books. The plots of the books and the Bond films leave out the routine side of the lives of real spies. However, some of Fleming's own exploits were as daring as those of the fictional agent 007.

# Types of spy

SPIES COME FROM many different backgrounds and either volunteer their services or are sought out and recruited by an espionage agency because they have access to secret information. Spies volunteering by walking into an embassy are called "walk-ins." Money is the most common tool used to attract spies in the world of espionage, but some are led by deeply held beliefs. Others spy because they are being blackmailed, and still more because it makes them feel important. A plant is a spy who is working or serving in a target organization and this way can penetrate (work their way into) a position where they can collect intelligence.

**TROUBADOURS**
These medieval minstrels went from castle to castle entertaining European nobles. Some spied by listening to royal gossip and repeating the news when they traveled to another country.

**CARELESS TALK**
Spies do not make themselves obvious by wearing uniforms! This wartime poster warned British citizens that they should not gossip about sons and husbands in the armed forces because "Careless talk costs lives." Bus passengers listening to the conversation might be spies and could report details of troop movements to the enemy.

*Walker tramped Vienna's streets while Soviet agents checked that he was not being followed*

*Building (indicated by red arrow on map) mentioned in Walker's typed instructions for a 1978 visit to Vienna*

**INSIDER TRAPPED**
French ambassador to Moscow Maurice Dejean unknowingly hired spies to work as his driver and maid. They used blackmail to try and turn him into an "agent in place." The plot failed, but Dejean's career was ruined.

**WALK-IN WALKER**
American John Walker worked for the US Navy and sold intelligence to the Soviet Union for 17 years. To meet them for payment and training, his Soviet handlers usually instructed Walker to travel to Vienna, Austria.

*The splendidly dressed Russian diplomats are "boyars"—members of noble Russian families*

## AMATEUR SPIES
Since Biblical times, traders have kept their eyes and ears open wide when they traveled abroad. These "amateur spies" are returning home from the land of Canaan to report what they had seen.

Iraq designed the "Supergun" to shell targets thousands of miles away

## SPIES AND SUPERWEAPONS
Although the United Nations attempts to ban international sale of munitions to certain countries, intelligence services often work in secret to supply weapons to countries they consider their friends. In the 1980s a Canadian, Gerald Bull, received the support of Western intelligence services as he supplied Iraq with parts for weapons such as this "supergun," which was intended to be capable of striking both Iran and Israel. Bull was assassinated in 1990.

## MOLE IN THE CIA
The nickname mole is given to serving intelligence officers who secretly work for another intelligence office—because they dig deep and work invisibly. Larry Wu Tai Chin, for example, was a CIA staff employee for more than 35 years and became a mole, spying for China.

## SPIES AT COURT
Espionage is against the law in every country, and if caught spies face prosecution and punishment. However, throughout history, diplomats, such as the well-dressed figures in this 16th-century woodcut, have been in a good position to spy and they are protected. These civil servants represent their country in its embassies abroad, and they have a license to spy. If they are caught, their diplomatic status protects them from punishment under international law. In fact, only very few work as spies. More are intelligence officers—they use their diplomatic jobs as a cover for recruiting and controlling agents who spy for them.

Procession of diplomats and merchants at the court of the Austrian archduke Maximilian II

# Secret toolkit

UNDERCOVER AGENTS OFTEN RELY ON AN ARRAY of sneaky tools, gadgets, and weapons. With these, a spy can bug a conversation or photograph a meeting. Other devices make escape easier or hide the evidence of espionage from prying eyes. Fictional spy James Bond made gadgets famous. Before a dangerous mission, he visited the workshop of "Q" who supplied him with ingenious devices. The character is based on the inventor Charles Fraser Smith (1904–1992), who designed the equipment for the British intelligence services in World War II. Although Bond author Fleming was acquainted with Fraser Smith, Q was not in the original Bond books and was added only in the movies. Other organizations had equally inventive spy workshops—for example, Stanley Lovell (1890–1976) supplied the American OSS (Office of Strategic Services) with gadgets during World War II.

A spoof spy kit for the wartime spy

Only slightly taller than a match

**SUPERSMALL SNAPPER**
Spies must be able to take photographs without attracting attention. This tiny digital camera concealed inside a cigarette lighter case was carried in a spy's pocket to be available when an opportunity arose to take a secret picture. Such camera concealments are only effective in areas where smoking is accepted and would be discovered if the lighter were closely examined during a search.

Lighter flips open to reveal camera

**HANDY HEEL**
Concealed items must be well hidden to escape discovery, and shoes and boots can hide fairly large weapons or tools. In World War II, spies sometimes concealed gold, for bribery, and knives in their insoles. Hidden weapons also came in handy for those taken captive.

Pen writes normally

Strip is pulled to withdraw concealed item

*Exposures lasted minutes, so fixed objects such as buildings were the only practical subjects*

*Acoustic tube to microphone*

### PINHOLE CAMERA
Some of the tiniest spy cameras use pinholes instead of a lens. KGB agents used this one in the 1980s. The camera takes pictures that are not blurred, however close or far away the object. However, nothing is really sharp either!

*...amera took ...ur pictures when ...gent uncovered ...e pinholes*

### LISTENING PEN
The circuits of radio transmitters are now so small that spies can install bugs in the tiniest of objects. This pen is inconspicuous in the pocket, and would not attract attention in a desk drawer. However, it conceals a microphone to eavesdrop on any nearby conversation. A tiny transmitter broadcasts the signal on UHF radio frequencies. The power of the signal is low, but strong enough for an accomplice who may be sitting in a car 1,600 ft (500 m) away to pick up the conversation with a receiver and record it.

*Body of pen conceals transmitter*

### A BRUSH WITH THE ENEMY
All spies risk capture, but the danger is perhaps even greater in wartime. So World War II spies hid all kinds of escape equipment in objects like this hairbrush. A compartment contains a saw to cut through prison bars, a map of enemy occupied territory, and a compass.

*Pulling bristles lifts compartment "lid"*

*Tube houses battery with enough power for up to six hours*

*Miniature saw blade*

*Compass*

*Compass needle*

Devices hidden in hairbrush

### EASY ACCESS
The safest way to enter a locked building is to bribe a low-paid employee to unlock the door. Where this is not possible, spies may try to pick the lock with specially shaped tools like these. In Britain, intelligence services employed a retired burglar to teach this vital skill to wartime agents.

*By inserting one of the hooked blades into a lock and turning gently, the tool lifts levers that hold the bolt in place*

*Map printed on thin paper to fold up small*

*Base of brush is hollow*

*Specially shaped instruments are called picklocks*

*Range of picklocks enables agent to tackle locks of different sizes*

*Picks fold away into penknife-like handle*

### CHEATING AT CARDS
In World War II escape maps concealed in a pack of playing cards were smuggled into Prisoner of War camps to help plan escapes. Tearing each card apart revealed a small area of the map. The map fit together like a jigsaw puzzle.

# Seeing the invisible

Visual surveillance is carried out by trained intelligence officers. They learn to use their eyes and cameras to collect intelligence, or for gathering information to blackmail their enemies. They use technology to make their vision keener. Magnifying lenses give a closer view of private scenes, while some night-vision equipment makes photography possible even in a candle-lit bedroom. However the clearest pictures do not guarantee the success of a surveillance mission. When spies secretly photographed a Western diplomat with his girlfriend, they were sure they could use the pictures for blackmail. They met the diplomat and threatened to send the pictures to his wife. His shameless response shocked them. "What wonderful shots!" he exclaimed. "Can you make me copies?"

**NOSY NEIGHBORS**
The well-equipped spy does not need to stretch to get a better view.

## ZOOMING IN
Sometimes spy agencies make use of commercially available equipment such as this high-resolution 35 mm camera with zoom lenses. The surveillance specialist photographs targets from long-distance either from a fixed observation post (OP) such as an apartment window or roof top, or a mobile OP (a car, or on foot). The purpose of a surveillance photo is to get intelligence information about a place, person, or activity (a clandestine meeting, exchange, or operation).

## CAUGHT IN THE ACT
To photograph subjects in near darkness, surveillance photography is carried out with either infrared film and a concealed infrared light source, or night-vision optics attached to the camera (opposite) using ambient light (light that already surrounds the object). Infrared light usually produces better photographs of documents or other targets, but it also might be detected by an alert counterspy. Ambient light is completely "passive" and undetectable, but since it does not record color, pictures have an eerie green glow.

Agent using a night-writing pen

Filters enhance image

Screen on back of camera allows user to check images taken before they leave the scene

Images are stored on a removable memory card inside the casing

An ordinary lens takes in the whole of the street market.

The powerful 300 mm lens picks out two particular figures from the crowd.

Two small batteries power goggles all night

Tubes make light 50,000 times brighter

Eyepieces adjust to suit the eyesight of individual spies

Zoom lens functions as a telescope

**SEEING IN THE DARK**
Night-vision goggles give spies the ability to see in very dim light. In total darkness an infrared flashlight casts a bright beam upon the scene for anyone wearing the goggles, but nothing can be seen by the target. Details differ, but most systems work like the image-forming tubes used on television cameras. The tube converts photons (packets of light) from the camera lens into electrons (tiny, electrically charged particles). The electrons speed toward a phosphor screen, making a brilliant glow where they strike it. The screen forms a brighter copy of the original

Twin lenses allow spy to judge distance

Lenses form life-size images so scene is not distorted and goggles can be used for night driving

Strong harness supports heavy goggles

Side view of night goggles

**ALL DONE WITH MIRRORS**
Spies in 19th-century France used these innocent-looking binoculars to keep a watch on their opponents. One lens produced the same view as an ordinary pair of binoculars. The other was a dummy. Behind it, an angled mirror gave a perfect view of whatever was happening to one side—while the spy appeared to be staring straight ahead. A similar device is still available today. Disguised as a lens hood, it enables spies to photograph subjects at their side, while pointing the camera forward.

Real lens

Focusing wheel

Dummy lens

Real lens inside

Hole for angled mirror

OH 1×20

# Bugs and taps

BEFORE YOU WHISPER "Tell me!" in a friend's ear, take a careful look around. Whispered words seem secret, but with bugs and wiretaps, spies can make sure that no conversation is really private. Like the insects they are named after, bugs are often tiny. They usually contain a microphone, power source, transmitter, and antenna. A spy who tunes a radio receiver to the correct frequency can hear every sound that reaches the bug, even if he or she is elsewhere. Telephone bugs or transmitters perform the same service each time a telephone is used. Digital (and tape) recorders make it easy to monitor wiretaps and bugs. When there is a sound, recording starts automatically, and the device stops after there have been a few moments of quiet.

**SENDING...**
A basic bug or transmitter can be very small indeed. This one is the size of a matchbox.

**...AND RECEIVIN**
This pocket-sized receiver picks u signals from the bug (left), relayin them to headphones or a tap recorder. The bug is a "quick plan type, small enough to hide behin a picture. Its battery lasts a wee The bug is cheap enough t abandon—returning to collect doubles the risk of discover

The 8-in (20-cm) bug found inside seal

**EMBASSY SEAL**
A gift from the Soviet Union, this replica eagle seal of the United States decorated that country's embassy in Moscow. In fact, the seal housed an ingenious bug. Sound made a spring inside the seal vibrate. Spies in a nearby building were able to detect the vibrations by using radar and interpret the words that caused the vibrations.

CIA microphone wristwatch

**WHAT IS THE TIME?**
This CIA wristwatch conceals a microphone. It is normally inconspicuous, but in 1977, a US embassy official in Moscow created suspicions about his diplomatic intentions when he visited KGB headquarters wearing two watches.

*Link to tape recorder hidden in agent's clothing*

**PHONE TAPPING**
Telephone taps can be easier to place than bugs because spies need not enter the room they want to listen to. Unless there is a switchboard, a telephone tap can go anywhere between the telephone and the exchange. In this film reconstruction from *Stakeout*, Chris Lecce (played by Richard Dreyfuss) uses a wiretap to keep a vital witness in an organized crime case under surveillance.

*Flexible antenna broadcasts call to listening spy or recorder*

*Fiber-optic light-sensing device*

*...ransmitter*

**TELEPHONE TRANSMITTER**
A telephone transmitter has the advantage that the "target" picks up the microphone and speaks directly and clearly into it! But the spy hears only the telephone calls, not any other speech in the room.

*Alligator clip connects to telephone line*

*Spy sets transmission frequency here*

*...ght-sensing ...vice causes ...nsmission to ...ut down when ...ceiver is replaced*

*Bug powered by lithium is harder to detect than bug that draws power from telephone line*

*Microprocessor unit picks up signals from light-sensing device and activates transmitter*

*Wiretap is connected directly to line*

**WIRETAP**
Sometimes a phone line can be tapped by connecting a couple of wires to leads in the junction box where the telephone line enters the building.

*Telephone tap connected by clips to a chosen line*

**TELEPHONE BUG**
In an office building where there are many extensions and a switchboard, a spy would need to install taps on every outside line and sift through many hours of tapes to hear just one short call. However, if a spy can enter the building unnoticed, a practical solution is possible—attaching a bug to a particular telephone. The spy can then either eavesdrop directly or record conversations and listen at leisure.

**MOBILE BUGS**
Modern cell phones are software-based and make it easier to be bugged by a clever adversary who sends a message containing a malicious code. Once received, the code takes over and allows conversations to be digitally monitored and retransmitted along with copies of the user's emails and files to the eavesdropper's secret internet site.

*The microphone may be activated remotely by spy software*

*A red dot reveals the user's position on the map*

**...EEPING IN TOUCH**
...ny time a cell phone is turned on, its location can ...e pinpointed by the authorities and the user's ...ovements tracked. Spies sometimes modify the ...oftware on cell phones to allow them secretly to ...onitor the location and travel route of their ...urveillance target. Then they can listen in and ...ollow their target through the phone.

*The software for GPS satellite positioning is built into most new cell phones*

# Listening in

Bugs do not always have a great range. The receiving distance is determined by the transmitting power, obstacles blocking the signal, and the level of radio interference from other radio users in the area. Lower power bugs are always desirable since the weaker signal is also harder for a counterintelligence service to detect and so locate the bug. The "listening post"—the receiving station—could be in an adjacent building, in a parked car, or even in the spy's pocket. The bug can be hidden in clothing if an agent has arranged a meeting with a contact in a street or park. Agents use cordless earphones and separate surveillance frequency to monitor and coordinate their activities surrounding the target area.

*Pin-sized antenna*

*If the microphone built into the case is plugged into the phone, then a switched-on cell phone resting inside a case can allow others to eavesdrop on or to record an encounter*

*Shirt hides induction loop, that picks up the conversation*

*Receiver can switch between two different bugs*

### BUG IN THE EAR

With wiring hidden under his shirt, an agent can monitor a bug without wearing conspicuous headphones. The listening device fits in the ear and looks like a hearing aid. The wire around the agent's neck creates an induction loop—a magnetic field that relays the amplified signal from a pocket receiver to the ear.

### WEARING A WIRE

The radio signal from a bug hidden in a spy's clothing can alert counterespionage agents operating bug detection equipment (pp. 48–49). A miniature recorder gets around the problem because it does not broadcast a radio signal.

*Wearer uses remote switch on microphone to activate it to record anything interesting*

### A BETTER RECEPTION

Although some general-purpose receivers can pick up bug signals, specially designed units are often more convenient and provide a better reception. This battery powered model links up with a portable recorder for unattended monitoring. An agent who set it up to receive signals from a telephone tap would need to return to the device only occasionally to change the tapes.

*Telescopic antenna*

*Car battery can power receiver for extended operation*

*Socket for headphones*

MON
CHANNEL   TAPE   MANUAL   TAPE   BATT
RUN    AUTO   POLARITY   LOW   Lorraine Electronics
LONDON
OFF
VOLUME
**UXR3**

## DIGITAL PEN
This pen is useful for more than taking notes—it is an unobtrusive way to record conversations and phone calls in an office, elevator, or perhaps an informal chat over lunch. Many pens download voice files straight on to a PC.

*Pen conceals a tiny digital recorder—some record for more than 12 hours and can be operated by remote control*

## STAKEOUT
Hidden microphones are legally used to investigate serious crimes and threats to national security. In the film *Stakeout* the head of security for a large American corporation listens in to a suspicious conversation. Laws limit the use of bugs, but some citizens' rights groups fear the controls are too weak.

*Bug is only 0.16 in (4 mm) thick and can hide behind a credit card, or nestle between pages of a datebook*

*Compartments in spine of case conceal the power supply and transmitter electronics*

*A digital voice recorder can store up to 70 hours of converstaions that can be downloaded directly to a computer*

*Pen contains minute bug*

## MAKING A CASE FOR BUGGING
Monitoring a meeting is a common task for both political and industrial spies. Digital recordings of conversations can provide evidence of unfair competition or help thwart a takeover by rivals. Bugging a briefcase is a discreet way to make a lasting record of "hush-hush" deals. Microphones built into a case can pick up speech on the far side of a room. It can be recorded or transmitted to a monitoring device outside. Touching the lock and a brass rivet head at the same time activates the device. Cell phones can be used to record or monitor conversations (pp. 14–15), and a bugged pen will attract no attention and allow the microphone to be close to the talker.

# Dropping in

HOMING PIGEONS have played an important part in intelligence work since the earliest days of espionage. Carrying a precious cargo of vital secrets, a spy's airborne courier, the homing pigeon, can soar high over enemy territory. Roman general Julius Caesar (100–44 BCE) used them to send intelligence messages during his campaigns in what is now France. Ever since, spies have valued the pigeon's speed and its ability to return home in almost any weather. More than half a million pigeons carried messages in World War I. Some even worked as spies— reconnaissance pigeons carried tiny cameras aloft to photograph enemy fortifications. In World War II, spies who located the launch sites of German "flying bombs" used pigeons as carriers to send the information to the Allied forces who bombed the sites.

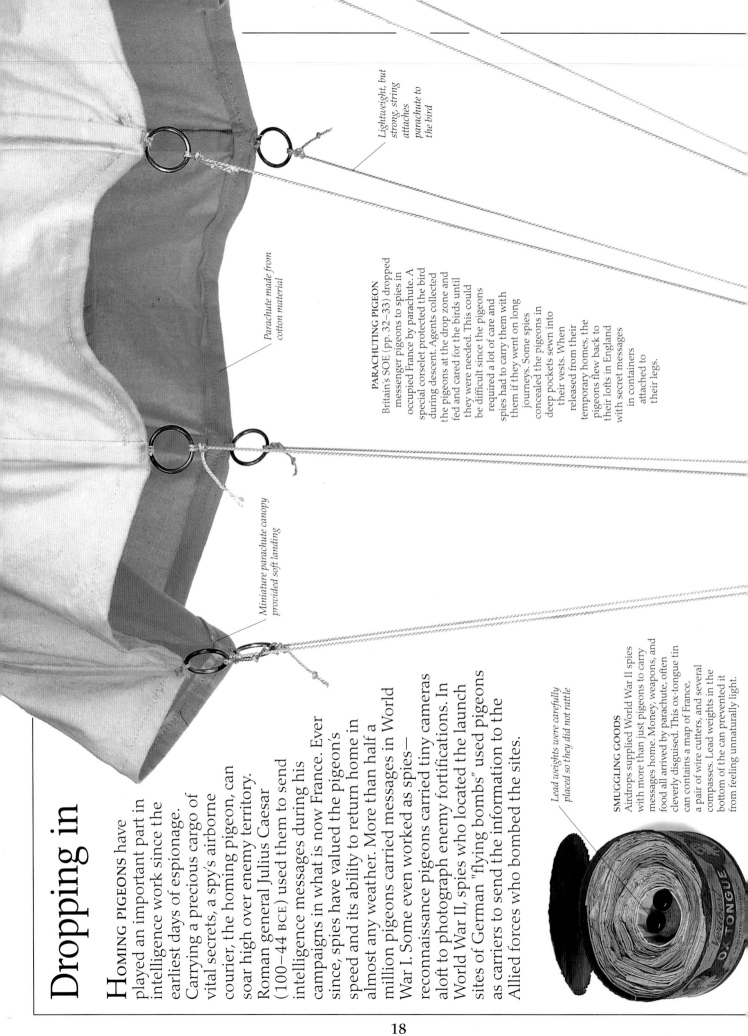

*Lightweight, but strong, string attaches parachute to the bird*

*Parachute made from cotton material*

*Miniature parachute canopy provided soft landing*

## PARACHUTING PIGEON

Britain's SOE (pp. 32–33) dropped messenger pigeons to spies in occupied France by parachute. A special corselet protected the bird during descent. Agents collected the pigeons at the drop zone and fed and cared for the birds until they were needed. This could be difficult since the pigeons required a lot of care and spies had to carry them with them if they went on long journeys. Some spies concealed the pigeons in deep pockets sewn into their vests. When released from their temporary homes, the pigeons flew back to their lofts in England with secret messages in containers attached to their legs.

*Lead weights were carefully placed so they did not rattle*

## SMUGGLING GOODS

Airdrops supplied World War II spies with more than just pigeons to carry messages home. Money, weapons, and food all arrived by parachute, often cleverly disguised. This ox-tongue tin can contains a map of France, a pair of wire cutters, and several compasses. Lead weights in the bottom of the can prevented it from feeling unnaturally light.

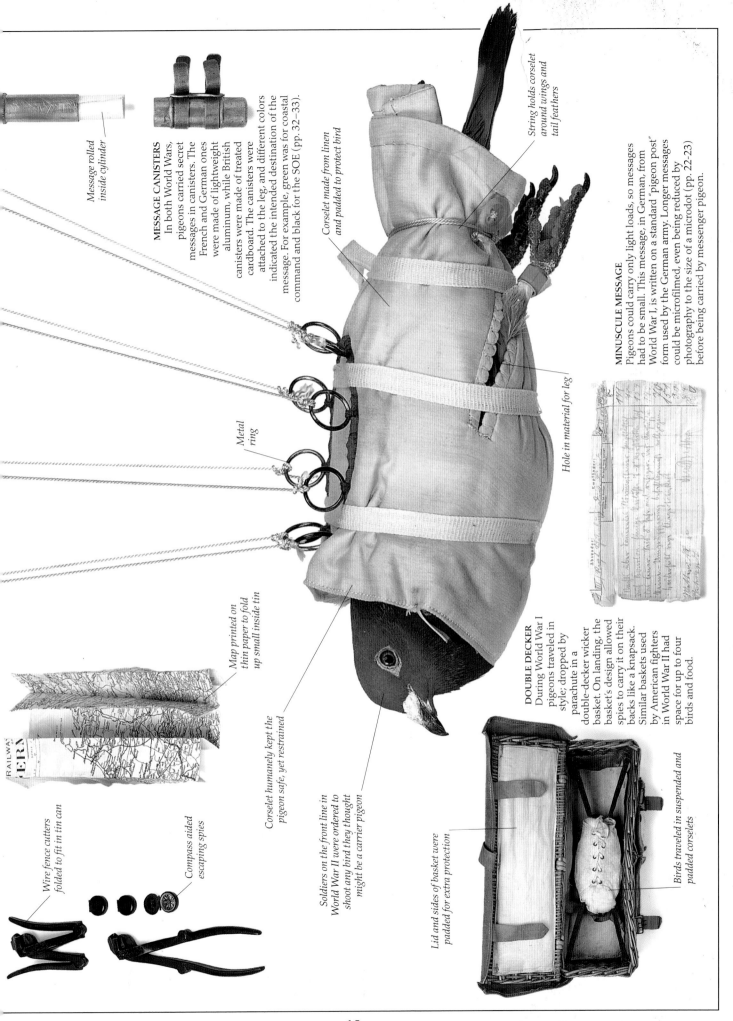

*Message rolled inside cylinder*

**MESSAGE CANISTERS**
In both World Wars, pigeons carried secret messages in canisters. The French and German ones were made of lightweight aluminum, while British canisters were made of treated cardboard. The canisters were attached to the leg, and different colors indicated the intended destination of the message. For example, green was for coastal command and black for the SOE (pp. 32–33).

*Corselet made from linen and padded to protect bird*

*String holds corselet around wings and tail feathers*

*Metal ring*

*Hole in material for leg*

**MINUSCULE MESSAGE**
Pigeons could carry only light loads, so messages had to be small. This message, in German, from World War I, is written on a standard "pigeon post" form used by the German army. Longer messages could be microfilmed, even being reduced by photography to the size of a microdot (pp. 22–23) before being carried by messenger pigeon.

*Map printed on thin paper to fold up small inside tin*

*Corselet humanely kept the pigeon safe, yet restrained*

*Wire fence cutters folded to fit in tin can*

*Compass aided escaping spies*

*Soldiers on the front line in World War II were ordered to shoot any bird they thought might be a carrier pigeon*

**DOUBLE DECKER**
During World War I pigeons traveled in style; dropped by parachute in a double-decker wicker basket. On landing, the basket's design allowed spies to carry it on their backs like a knapsack. Similar baskets used by American fighters in World War II had space for up to four birds and food.

*Lid and sides of basket were padded for extra protection*

*Birds traveled in suspended and padded corselets*

# Animal spies

In the past hundred years, military and intelligence services have sometimes trained animals to support and even replace the work of human agents or soldiers. Animals can make ideal spies, since they are rarely viewed with suspicion and tend to be overlooked because they blend in with the surroundings. Typically, they are trained to deliver secret messages or carry out reconnaissance missions, but sometimes they perform tasks beyond the capabilities of humans, such as laying bugging wires through drainpipes or tracking enemy agents by their scent. In the 1970s, the CIA experimented with robotic dragonflies, and today scientists are trying to use microchip-implants to turn live moths into miniature surveillance devices capable of being controlled remotely.

**SPIES WITH WINGS**
During World War I, pigeons not only acted as secret message carriers (pp. 18–19) but also carried out aerial reconnaissance missions. The birds were trained to fly along specific routes and then released carrying tiny spring-driven motorized cameras that took photos automatically at preset intervals. They returned with images of the terrain along the route, revealing the location of enemy forces.

**MESSENGER DOGS**
Pigeons were not the only animals employed as messengers in World War I. Here, a German messenger dog leaps over a trench in 1917. Dogs could cover the ground two or three times faster than a person and get through when it was too dark for signaling, or too foggy, wet, or dark for pigeons.

*Microphone in ear canal*

*Wire antenna woven into fur*

*Transmitter and battery*

**OPERATION ACOUSTIC KITTY**
In 1961, the CIA surgically implanted electronic devices into a female cat to turn her into a mobile bugging device. The plan was to teach Acoustic Kitty, as she became known, to follow a specific route that would take her to within eavesdropping distance of an Asian head of state. The technology worked fine, but in training Kitty all too often wandered off the route. The project was abandoned, the devices removed, and Kitty lived out the rest of her life as a normal (nonspy) cat.

**ANTISUBMARINE SEAGULLS**
In World War I, British admiral Sir Frederick Inglefield wanted to train seagulls to defecate on the periscopes of German U-boat submarines to "blind" them. Dummy periscopes were set up in Poole Harbour, Dorset, England, but the birds proved uncooperative. During World War II, the US Navy considered using seagulls to reveal the location of U-boats. By coating dummy periscopes with fish oil, it was thought that the birds might be trained to fly patrols off the US coast and land on the periscopes of submarines lurking offshore. The plan was never followed up.

**CIA DEAD RAT DROPS**
To pass secret communications to agents in Moscow, the CIA used dead rats that had been disemboweled to create a storage cavity in their stomachs. Money, film, and secret cipher material could be hidden in the cavity and the rat left on a Moscow street for retrieval by an agent. When hungry cats began eating the rats before they could be recovered, the CIA doused the rats in hot-pepper sauce to deter them!

## SCENT TRACKERS

In the Cold War, East Germany's Stasi trained male German Shepherd dogs to track hormone scents secreted by female dogs. The scents were placed on the doormats of suspected spies to contaminate their shoes. The dogs could then track the targets through the East Berlin streets for up to three days. Other methods used sterile cloths to capture a person's scent from their car seat or where they had been standing. Kept in an airtight jar, the scent samples stayed "fresh" and could be used for tracking years later.

Jar of scent samples from the Stasi museum in Berlin

## RODENT AGENT

Officers from MI6, the British intelligence service, once used a mouse to help bug the apartment of a suspected Russian spy in Lisbon, Portugal. MI6 agents trained the mouse to carry a radio wire from a microphone in the loft through the bends in a drainpipe to a receiver in an apartment below the suspect's home.

## DRAGONFLY IMPERSONATOR

The Insectothopter was a miniature UAV (Unmanned Aerial Vehicle) developed by the CIA's research and development office during the 1970s to eavesdrop on conversations. This robot bug was the size of a dragonfly and was handpainted to look like one. The four wings were powered by a tiny gasoline engine. The Insectothopter was test-flown in 1976, but the project was abandoned when the Insectothopter was found to be too difficult to control in crosswinds.

*Robot bug was designed to hover outside windows.*

## FINNED AGENTS

The US Navy uses specially trained dolphins and sea lions to patrol harbors in search of mines, enemy spies, and saboteurs who might be trying to plant explosives on the hulls of US ships. The dolphins can also be trained to photograph the secret design of a foreign ship's hull. There have been claims that the Navy has even tried equipping dolphins with poison-dart guns that could be fired underwater to stop enemy-agent divers, although the Navy denies this.

*Sphinx moth*

## BIONIC MOTHS

US government scientists have experimented with implanting microcomputers into a sphinx moth in an attempt to control its movements and use the moth to collect and transmit data. Electronic sensors convert the moth's muscle vibrations into power for the onboard microcomputer. The plan is eventually to mount the bugs with surveillance equipment for use in reconnaissance missions too risky for human agents.

# Secret messages

Spies rely on fast, secure communications. Speed is crucial because intelligence quickly loses its value, and secrecy is essential to protect the messages sent and the spy. Using radio, spies could communicate over long distances almost instantly. However, anyone tuning to the right wavelength was able to intercept radio messages. With three receivers counterintelligence agents were able to triangulate, or pinpoint, a hidden transmitter in minutes and capture the spy. Today, a modern cell phone connected to the internet can duplicate all of the secret communications capabilities of the devices shown on this page.

Headphones allowed agent to listen to broadcasts without others hearing them

Transmitter works from socket or battery power

Apparatus packs into a suitcase and weighs 32 lb (14.5 kg)

Oluf Reed Olsen's code sheets

Headphone connector

Frequency dial

Voltage adjuster

O. Reed Olsen.

KONFIDENTIELLT.

INSTRUKSJONEM

FOR BRUK AV

TYPE SS-TR 1 SMÅ R/MOTTAGERSETT.

N.B. LES DISSE INSTRUKSJONER GODT GJENNEM
FØR DU PRØVER AA BRUKE SETTET.

**HUMAN SIGNALS**
Spies sometimes take desperate risks to carry intelligence. This World War I Belgian courier carried a message written on her back in invisible ink. Unfortunately, the ruse did not succeed: her captors discovered the message and executed the courier.

Spare valve

*Crystal plugs in to change transmission frequency*

*Antenna—a 60-ft (18-m) length of wire—plugs in here*

*Terminals attached to car battery for transmission without mains power*

*Spare tubes were carried in this compartment*

*Tapping key sends coded messages as long and short pulses of radio waves*

## NORWEGIAN SECRET AGENT

When German forces invaded neutral Norway in 1940, Oluf Reed Olsen fled the country in a sailboat. Reaching Britain, he trained as a radio operator, returning to Norway in 1943, where spies in the Kristiansand naval base supplied him with details of German shipping movements. Olsen coded the messages and transmitted them to Britain from a camouflaged camp hidden in the trees above the harbor at Kristiansand. He used the radio set shown here. The cipher was considered unbreakable because it was based on sets of random numbers of which Reed Olsen and MI6 held the only copies.

Oluf Reed Olsen using the suitcase radio at his camouflaged base in 1944

*Message can be reduced until it is the size of a period*

MICRODOTS
Photography provides agents with a simple way to send messages secretly. By photographing a document with a special camera, a spy can produce a microdot—a negative that is 100 times smaller than the original. This paragraph about microdots can be reduced to a microdot the size of a period and then hidden in a perfectly innocent letter. The agent who receives the letter can read every word of the microdot with the help of a microscope.

## CONVICTED BY RADIO

Peter and Helen Kroger hid a radio transmitter under the kitchen floor of their house. With it they transmitted British submarine secrets to Russia. They chose a house in west London, England, close to three busy airports, hoping that communications between aircraft and control towers would hide their secret signals. At their trial in 1961, the radio was used as evidence.

## DOTTY PHOTOGRAPHY

Microdot cameras can be simple in construction, and small enough to hide easily. However, microphotography is difficult to do. Unless agents are very careful with the exposure of the film and its processing, the dot will be impossible to read.

Microdot camera (actual size)

## MICRODOTS

Photography provides agents with a simple way to send messages secretly. By photographing a document with a special camera, a spy can produce a microdot—a negative that is 100 times smaller than the original. This paragraph about microdots can be reduced to a microdot the size of a period and then hidden in a perfectly innocent letter. The agent who receives the letter can read every word of the microdot with the help of a microscope.

# Codes and ciphers

ESPIONAGE AGENTS use "codes" and "ciphers" to communicate and keep their messages secret. In codes, letters, numbers, or symbols replace either the words or the entire meaning of a message or signal. Some codes are in general use. For example, when you mail a letter, a zipcode guides it to the right destination. Spies sometimes send messages in Morse code—dots and dashes that all radio operators understand. Other codes and ciphers are very complicated and difficult to break. Ciphers are a type of code but they have a secret "key" for encrypting the message—translating it into a cipher. The key can be a number, a word, even a poem. Anyone who has been given the key can easily decrypt the signal—change it back to plain text. Without knowing the key, the message reads as nonsense.

**SIMPLE CIPHER**
Ciphers do not need to be complicated if it is important only to hide their meaning from a casual glance. This jolly figure from World War I spells out "Ypres" (the site in Belgium of a famous battle) and a date, the "8th."

**CIPHER DISK**
This metal cipher disk, invented in 1802, is less than 2½ in (6 cm) in diameter. The two inner circles are rotated to align with different letters and numbers on the outer two circles. This produces a simple, easily broken substitution cipher in which each letter stands for another, so "W," for example, represents "E" whenever it occurs.

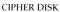
*Code sheet is tiny so Yvonne Cormeau could easily hide it*

**CODE SHEETS**
Charts like these convert a commonly used operational phrase into a coded word. It saves time and effort for the agent. These miniature code sheets were hidden in the handbag of SOE wireless operator Yvonne Cormeau in World War II (pp. 32–33). When she used a chart for Morse transmissions, a different letter would replace "E" each time it occurred in the message.

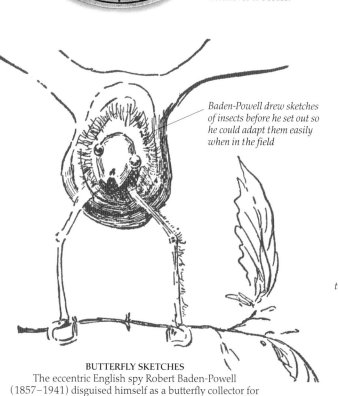

*Baden-Powell drew sketches of insects before he set out so he could adapt them easily when in the field*

**BUTTERFLY SKETCHES**
The eccentric English spy Robert Baden-Powell (1857–1941) disguised himself as a butterfly collector for one of his intelligence-gathering missions in Montenegro, on the coast of the Adriatic Sea. While he was there, he sketched this specimen of a moth perched on a twig.

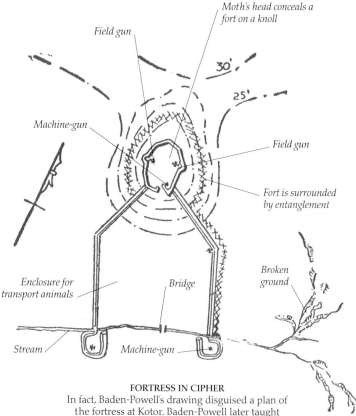

*Moth's head conceals a fort on a knoll*

*Field gun*

*Machine-gun*

30'

25'

*Field gun*

*Fort is surrounded by entanglement*

*Enclosure for transport animals*

*Bridge*

*Broken ground*

*Stream*

*Machine-gun*

**FORTRESS IN CIPHER**
In fact, Baden-Powell's drawing disguised a plan of the fortress at Kotor. Baden-Powell later taught espionage skills to the children in the Boy Scout movement that he founded in 1908.

## ROYAL CIPHER

Mary Queen of Scots (1542–1587) encrypted messages to allies outside her prison walls (pp. 28–29). In the substitution cipher that they used, the same symbol stood for a letter each time it appeared, so that the cipher was easy to break.

*Numbers between the symbols represented people's names*

*Coded letter signed by Anthony Babington, conspirator in a plot to assassinate Elizabeth I*

*Lid holds spare light bulbs*

*Bulbs lit behind lettered windows on the lid to indicate enciphered character*

*Positions of rotors controlled encryption of each letter*

*Rotors spun after each letter, ensuring that cipher pattern never repeated*

*Cipher was keyed in*

*Connecting sockets with plugs made the cipher more complicated*

*Rotors and plugs gave several million million combinations*

Klappe schließen

## SPEEDING UP ENCRYPTION

The Enigma cipher machine was used by German soldiers (above), and diplomats to aid intelligence in the 1930s and during World War II. The signals baffled enemy cryptanalysts (cipher experts) who intercepted them and tried to break the cipher. The Polish secret service, with the help of a recruited spy in the German cipher office, was able to interpret three-quarters of the Enigma messages by 1938, and in 1939 passed on this knowledge to Britain and France.

## ENIGMA IN OPERATION

After setting plugs and three or four rotors, encryption on Enigma was automatic. Pressing a letter key lit up a different letter on the display above. The encrypted letter was different each time. Decryption on the receiving Enigma machine reversed the process. In principle, coded messages from the Enigma machine were impossible to read without knowing the rotor and plug settings. But that information and an actual Enigma machine supplied by the Polish Secret Service helped the British break most of the Enigma codes in an operation called "Ultra," which remained secret until 1972.

# Intercepts and code-breaking

CIPHERS HELP PROTECT secret messages, but they do not destroy the meaning completely. Like a word puzzle, the sense of the message remains locked inside. An enemy who intercepts the signal will try hard to find the key. Intelligence agencies employ code-breakers called cryptanalysts to do this. With a substitution cipher (pp. 24–25), a cryptanalyst starts by counting letters. In English, "E" is used more often than other letters. So, if in the message "W" appears most, it probably stands for "E." The next step is to look for two-letter words ending in "E." There are only four in English: he, me, be, and we. Then the cryptanalyst will look for letters that stand on their own—in English there are just two one-letter words, "A" and "I." With techniques like these and even more complex ones, cryptanalysts can solve elaborate cipher puzzles, although it can sometimes take them a long time. Computers speed the process, but cryptanalysts need to be very patient. Few though, are as patient as a 17th-century Arab who deciphered a message to the Sultan of Morocco. It took him 16 years.

**CIPHER CLERKS AT WORK**
Britain's code-breaking center in World War II was at Bletchley Park near London, set up in August 1939. More than 5,000 staff worked on up to 2,000 encrypted messages a day.

**ZIMMERMANN TELEGRAM**
Deciphered in Britain in 1916, this telegram was sent by the Germans to their ambassador in Mexico. It suggested that Mexico form an alliance with Germany and invade three southern US states. The interception of the telegram was possibly the most important spying event of the war. Shocked Americans quickly entered World War I on Britain's side.

Polish inventors named machine after the ice-cream "bombe" they were eating at the time

WRENS (members of the Women's Royal Navy) operated the machines

**GOING LIKE A BOMBE**
Cryptanalysts at the code-breaking center at Bletchley Park used some of the first computers to help them break codes and ciphers. In two hours, a "bombe" could try every combination of rotor positions that was in use on the Enigma machines that Germany was using. A later machine, called Colossus, was the world's first electronic computer, a forerunner of the laptops in use today.

Bombe simply stopped when it broke the cipher

Japanese aircraft bomb Pearl Harbor, December 7, 1941

USS West Virginia *ablaze after suffering two aerial bombs and seven torpedo hits*

### THE PURPLE MACHINE
Like Enigma (pp. 24–25), the Japanese Purple cipher machine used a plug board to create a huge number of possible keys. However, Purple used telephone switches in place of the rotors found in Enigma. A team of US cryptanalysts, including William Friedman (below left), cracked the Purple cipher by building a replica of the mechanism.

### PEARL HARBOR PREDICTIONS
By cracking the Purple code (right), American cipher experts predicted a Japanese attack on December 7, 1941, but could not name the hour or the place. The spy Dusko Popov (pp. 56–57) had a microdot that contained intelligence questions about Pearl Harbor and Richard Sorge (pp. 34–35) had predicted that Japan would attack southward. The intelligence wasn't enough—the devastating surprise raid took place on Pearl Harbor in Hawaii at 6:00 a.m, when many US servicemen were still asleep. The attack killed 2,300 Americans, crippled the American fleet, and drew the United States into World War II.

### HUSBAND AND WIFE TEAM
Russian-born American William F. Friedman (1891–1969) led the US Army Signals Intelligence Service team that cracked Japan's Purple cipher. Friedman worked on ciphers during both world wars. In the 1920s, his wife Elizebeth broke the codes of rum smugglers during prohibition, when alcohol was banned in the United States.

### PIONEERING CRYPTANALYST
Herbert Osborne Yardley (1889–1958) was a brilliant cryptanalyst and pioneered code-breaking for the United States during World War I and afterward. He set up the US unit that became known as the "Black Chamber" to read foreign intelligence material. His work in the 1920s was later used to help break the Purple cipher.

Herbert Yardley's security pass

### THE "DEAD SOLDIER"
In 1943, the drowned body of a British major was washed ashore in Spain. Papers he was carrying described plans by the Allies to attack Greece and Sardinia, and German troops immediately moved there. In fact, "Major Martin" was actually a civilian who had died of pneumonia. Intelligence chiefs had arranged for his body to be dressed as a soldier and pushed from a submarine off the Spanish coast. The Germans were completely taken in, and when they moved their troops, they left very few soldiers on Sicily—the Allies' real target.

Planted theater ticket stubs made the major's story appear genuine

"Major Martin's" fake identity card planted by intelligence officers

*Photograph of living person who looked like "Major Martin"*

# Concealment

*Wrist strap*

*Right-angle viewfinder*

*Lens*

*Direct vision viewfinder*

*Setting for bright light*

*Aperture setting knob*

A CLOAK AND DAGGER are the traditional trademarks of the secret agent. The spy hides the dagger, the badge of the assassin, under the cloak, which stands for secrecy, disguise, and concealment. Spies of the past could put on a cloak quickly to hide their true identity. Some chose more exotic disguises—Louis XV's agent the Chevalier d'Eon dressed as a woman for many years. For a modern spy, disguise is just as necessary, but much more subtle. Today's agents try to look ordinary, aiming to pass unnoticed in a crowd. Agents also choose ordinary-looking objects as hiding places. Hidden in a working battery, a secret message is safe from even a close inspection. By miniaturizing their messages, spies can conceal them in even smaller objects. Large objects are more difficult to hide. But an ingenious and determined spy can hide heavy equipment, tank engines—even kidnapped people.

**SPY RING**
Microdots (pp. 22–23) reduce documents to the size of a period. In World War II, British agents hid them in this hollow ring.

**ROYAL BEER BARREL**
Imprisoned by England's Queen Elizabeth I, Mary, Queen of Scots (1542–1587) smuggled messages to sympathizers in a beer barrel. She wrapped encrypted documents in a waterproof bag, probably an animal bladder. Then she pushed the bag through the stopper hole into the barrel. Replies traveled back into her prison by the same route. Her "postman," a double agent named Gilbert Gifford, betrayed the scheme (p. 41).

*Wooden stopper seals barrel when full of beer*

*Mary, Queen of Scots*

**SMILE PLEASE!**
"Detective" cameras disguised as books, hats, and neckties first appeared in the 1880s. As early as 1893 spies were taking pictures with cameras shaped like pocket watches. This wristwatch camera dates from 1948. On its 1-inch (25-mm) diameter disk of film it takes eight pictures, each the size of a fingernail.

*Cell provides 1.5 volt power*

*Compartment is big enough to hold a roll of film*

*Magnet grips base to unscrew it*

**DIGITAL ROCK SPY**
Spies leave messages in prearranged hiding-places, or "dead drops." Leaving a message at a dead drop is safer than arranging to meet an agent in person. British Intelligence used this digital dead drop inside a fake rock to receive, store, and retransmit messages to an agent in Moscow. Other digital dead drops can be created over the internet from anywhere in the world.

*Three round flat batteries provided power for the electronic circuitry*

*Small integrated circuits communicated secretly with the agent's cell phone*

*The fake rock was hidden by a busy road*

**BATTERIES INCLUDED**
This ingenious hiding place looks like a normal battery, and a cell inside provides enough power to light a bulb. However, there is a secret compartment at the base.

Dukes as Comrade
Piotrovsky

Dukes as an ailing
intellectual

Dukes as a bearded
worker

Dukes as an epileptic

*Contemporary
print of the
Chevalier d'Eon*

*D'Eon complained
that he sometimes
forgot whether he
was wearing a
woman's headdress
or a man's helmet*

**A SHADY LADY**
The Chevalier d'Eon
(1728–1810) was an expert
fencer and lawyer. He began his
career as a spy for French king
Louis XV in 1756. He posed as
a shy woman in the Russian
court to gain the confidence of
the Russian empress
and also worked as
a double agent for
the British. He
lived in London
as a female at the
end of his life and
when he died many
people were
shocked to learn
his real identity.

**AGENT ST 25**
Paul Dukes became an expert in
disguise as head of British
intelligence in Russia. He was in
Moscow in 1917 when revolution
swept the communists to power.
Pursued by the Cheka (secret
police), Dukes brashly
posed as Comrade
Piotrovsky, a Cheka
officer. To the British, he
was "Agent ST 25."

*Clamps held
ankles and neck*

*Small seat*

**HOW TO SMUGGLE A SPY**
In 1964, drugged and bundled in
a trunk, Israeli Mordecai Louk
narrowly escaped being
exported from Rome to Cairo
disguised as diplomatic mail.
He was freed when a customs
guard heard the box
whimper. Louk had
been spying in
Italy for the
Egyptians.

*Leather
slots for feet*

*Trunk was only
53 in (137 cm) long*

# Spies at war

Advancing armies rely on expert soldiers to survey the land ahead and judge the enemy's strength. However, not all are spies. Some are scouts who work openly and wear army uniforms. If they are caught, they spend the rest of the war in prison. Wartime spies, though, disguise themselves to avoid capture, and they collect information secretly. So anyone caught in enemy territory wearing the clothes of a civilian can be tried as a spy, and the punishment—usually execution—is immediate. Despite this harsh penalty, spies have operated in almost every war. The 18th-century German king, Frederick the Great, even bragged about the number he employed. Mocking a French commander as a gourmet, he joked "A hundred cooks follow him—but ahead of me go a hundred spies!"

Major Coleridge's diary, July 13, 1899

**SOUTHERN BELLE**
Many women worked as spies in the Civil War (1861–1865) and Belle Boyd (1844–1900) became one of the most famous Confederate (Southern) agents. She learned military secrets from Union (Northern) officers lodged in her Virginia home and braved gunfire to tell Confederate leaders. After capture and then release in a prisoner exchange, she received a heroine's welcome in the South.

**DEATH OF A SPY**
Major John André (1751–1780) was hanged as a spy during the Revolutionary War (1775–1783). He had gone to meet US traitor Benedict Arnold (1741–1801), the commander of West Point, a fortress that guarded the Hudson River Valley. Arnold wanted to surrender the fort to the British, and he handed André details of his plans. The ship that was to take André and the secret plans back to the British Army was fired on and left without him. André disguised himself as a civilian, but was caught by the American militia with the secret papers hidden in his boots. The British spy was hanged in 1780.

**DETECTIVE SPYMASTER**
When civil war divided the United States, Abraham Lincoln turned to a private detective to help gather intelligence for the Union army. The choice seemed to be a natural one—the Scotsman Allan Pinkerton (1819–1884), head of the famous detective agency, had already foiled one attempt to assassinate President Lincoln. Unfortunately, Pinkerton knew very little about war, and his agents were often clumsy and sometimes cowardly. He resigned as Lincoln's spymaster in 1862

Hollow bullet used by Major
Coleridge to hide his

## FIGHTING THE BOERS

In the Boer War (1899–1902) British forces fought to control farms and gold in what is now South Africa. Their enemies, the Afrikaners, or Boers, were descendants of white Dutch settlers. Major H. F. Coleridge was among those who spied for the British, and his diaries (left) record details of the Boer defenses. The British intelligence service did not realize the value of the intelligence that spies like Coleridge supplied, and he had to plead for more money to continue his work (below).

### CARTOON CAPTURE
During World War I (1914–1918), spies usually operated far from the front line, in neutral nations such as Switzerland and the Netherlands (Holland). Nevertheless, the public fear of spies and their exploits inspired many cartoons. This colorful example shows a German spy captured by French troops.

*Coleridge sent this
telegram asking for
more money in 1900*

*French-born
Violette Szabo
was the best shot
in Britain's SOE*

### COURAGEOUS COMMANDO
Violette Szabo was fluent in French and a skillful rifle shooter—London shooting galleries banned her because she always hit the target—perfect qualifications for a spy. She was approached by the SOE (Special Operations Executive) during World War II (1939–1945) and agreed, to avenge the death of her husband Etienne (above), who died fighting for the British in north Africa. She was admired by fellow spies for her courage and determination. She was captured after a gun battle on her second SOE mission in France, when she was sabotaging telegraph lines. Violette Szabo was executed in a German prison camp.

*Lincoln (center) dismissed
his general (left) after the
disaster at Antietam*

*On September 17, 1862, 12,000
Union troops died at the battle
of Antietam, largely due to
bad intelligence, and
Pinkerton (right)
resigned*

### TOO GOOD TO BE TRUE
The most clever agent of World War II, codenamed "Cicero," was extremely good at spying for Germany. He was an Albanian and his real name was Elyesa Bazna. While working as valet to the British ambassador in Turkey, he opened the embassy safe and photographed secret codes, lists of British spies, and the Allied plans to invade Europe. But these documents were so secret that the German leaders could not believe they were genuine and ignored Cicero. Nevertheless, they paid him a fortune in banknotes—but all of them were forgeries.

# A cover story

**BITTER PILL**
Some SOE agents carried a suicide L-pill (lethal pill) that would kill in seconds. No agent ever used it.

**D**ISGUISED AS A CHILD'S NURSE, "Annette" passes through a wartime roadblock in southwest France. "Annette," who is really the radio operator Yvonne Cormeau, tells her cover story well, escaping capture for a year and transmitting over 400 coded messages. During World War II, the lives of many secret agents depended on their cover stories—invented pasts designed to hide their real identity. In Britain, the Special Operations Executive (SOE) trained agents, giving them cover stories that they learned by heart. Then the SOE dropped the agents in France by parachute or small boat.

Fake French matchbox

**POCKET KNIFE**
Male and female agents carried pocket knives to help with sabotage, if necessary, such as slicing through an enemy's car tires.

**VITAL TIMING**
A late arrival usually signaled danger. Cautious agents did not wait more than a few minutes at a rendezvous.

**PARTING GIFT**
SOE agents were given a valuable present such as this silver cigarette case before leaving on a mission. The gift could be used as a bribe if an agent was caught by a corrupt official.

*Wallet*

*Powder compact*

**MINI-MAPS**
War agents used maps to plan sabotage. A silk map (above) folds very small to aid concealment.

*Mirror*

**TINY TAPPER**
A Morse code key was small enough to hide easily in a handbag.

**PLUG-IN TUNING**
Yvonne Cormeau carried a variety of crystals. She could change them to tune her SOE radio to the correct wavelength.

*Code sheets*

**HANDBAG HIDING PLACE**
Between the lining and outer skin of Yvonne Cormeau's handbag is the secret compartment in which she hid code sheets (pp. 24–25) and a transmission schedule.

The clothes had to be tailored in the French style of the 1940s

SOE carefully removed all English labels before sending an agent into enemy territory

Every detail of clothing reinforced the cover story—an agent posing as a clerk would wear a simple, inexpensive hat like this one

Yvonne Cormeau's tattered leather briefcase

Briefcase fit in with one of Yvonne Cormeau's disguises—a district nurse

**YVONNE CORMEAU, SOE RADIO OPERATOR**
Many of these items belonged to Yvonne Cormeau, the SOE agent whose cover name was "Annette." She parachuted in to France on the night of August 22–23, 1943, and worked as a radio operator. Her natural caution helped her to keep from being captured until Allied forces liberated France in 1944. On one occasion, she recognized another agent on a train but resisted the temptation to speak—she had learned in training that if he was under suspicion, they might both be captured. On the other hand, Yvonne Cormeau knew when it was worth taking a risk. Although most radio operators moved their radio sets daily to avoid capture, she felt safe transmitting from the same house for six months. From the windows she could spot interception vans over 3 miles (5 km) away.

Stockings could be used as a bribe by the SOE agent as silk was very rare in wartime

Suede shoes

# Agents, moles, and defectors

**TRIBUTE TO A SPY**
Richard Sorge (1895–1944) appeared to be a fanatical Nazi during World War II. While a political adviser to the German ambassador, he was feeding secrets to Germany's Russian enemies. Soviet stamps showed Sorge as a hero.

DOUBLE AGENTS ARE REALLY "controlled enemy agents." Rather than serving two masters they work for only one side in a war of espionage—but they deceive the other side into thinking they are working for them and instead steal their secrets. Being a double agent is very risky. To be successful they must develop the trust of an intelligence agency, while their sole goal is to betray that trust. If caught they can expect no mercy in their punishment. Double agents may be volunteers, or they could be spies unmasked by counterintelligence agencies who have been "turned" (recruited and controlled) rather than prosecuted. Their new masters provide them with false but believable information, and the spy passes on the bogus secrets as if they were true.

Defectors are intelligence officers who leave their home country to go to another country and reveal the secrets brought with them. Although they may be admired in the country to which they are truly loyal, they earn hatred in the country they betrayed.

Aldrich and Rosario Ames after their separate trials for spying

**ANCIENT SPYMASTER**
Chinese commander Sun Tzu was among the first to write about double agents. He called them "doomed spies"—who do certain things openly for purposes of deception and allow our spies to report them to the enemy. Sun Tzu wrote his book, *The Art of War*, in the 4th century BCE.

**RUSSIAN AGENT AT THE CIA**
For nine years Aldrich Ames (born 1941) was a Soviet spy while working as a trusted officer at the CIA. Ames and his wife, Rosario, provided details of many spies recruited by the CIA and, with their help, Moscow was able to build a network of double agents who deceived their CIA bosses. The pair were paid well by the Russians for their treachery.

# ЗДРАВСТВУЙТЕ, ТОВАРИЩ ФИЛБИ

«Если бы мне предстояло начать жизнь сызнова, я начал бы так, как начал».

**Феликс ДЗЕРЖИНСКИЙ.**

ДЕКАБРЬСКОЕ морозное утро, ноч- ная мгла еще не ушла с засне- женных улиц. Деревья на Гоголевском бульваре покрыты пушистым инеем. У троллейбусной остановки — цепочка по-

представить все, что угодно. Предпо- ложить, что в то августовское утро в ка- бинете за столом напротив него сидел кадровый сотрудник советской разведки, он не мог даже в дурном сне.

— Я делал, что мог в то время, и был счастлив узнать однажды, что я зачис- лен в кадры советской разведки.

— Каким же образом, товарищ Ким, вам удалось попасть на службу в анг- лийскую разведку?

— Это довольно длинная история, — говорит он. — После окончания Кэмбрид- жа я некоторое время работал в одной

— Я пошел вверх по служебной лест- нице. Через год я уже был заместите- лем начальника одного из отделов МИ-6.

— МИ-6, что это значит?

— В Англии существует две службы: под кодовым названием МИ-5 скрывает- ся контрразведка. МИ-6 — это собствен- но секретная разведывательная служба.

— Западная пресса отмечала, что ва-

Он был внимателен в обращении с людь- ми, но по существу относился к ним свысока. В дела он не вникал, и, я бы сказал, при всей его агрессивности он был дилетантом, о чем лучше всего го- ворит авантюра с вторжением на Кубу, чем позорно провалившись. Считают, что он занял этот пост благодаря сво- ему брату — Джону Фостеру Даллесу.

## HERO'S WELCOME
Philby escaped to Moscow from Beirut, where he had been working under cover as a journalist. The Soviet newspapers welcomed him with banner headlines. This one reads "Greetings Comrade Philby."

## COLD WAR MOLE
Harold "Kim" Philby (1912–1988) became a communist while he was studying at Cambridge University, and was a Soviet spy by 1933. Yet, seven years later, he had a job with Britain's MI6 intelligence service. After thirty years of spying he fled to Moscow. A grateful Soviet Union gave him a pension and an apartment, the office of which is shown above.

## MEDALS FROM BOTH SIDES
Philby received this plaque from the KGB soon after his arrival in Moscow. Later the Soviet Union gave him the Order of the Red Banner. Eighteen years before, England's King George VI, unaware that he was a spy, had given Philby the Order of the British Empire.

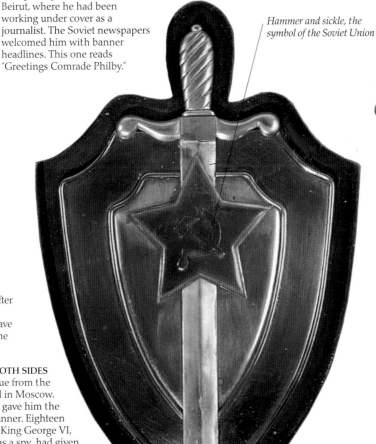

*Hammer and sickle, the symbol of the Soviet Union*

## RETIREMENT IN MOSCOW
After defecting, Philby lived in Moscow until his death in 1988. His son took this photograph of him in the 1970s. The treachery of Philby and his fellow spies Guy Burgess and Donald Maclean left behind a trail of mistrust. Their espionage discredited the British intelligence services.

## SECURITY SECRETS
As head of the KGB mission in London, Oleg Gordievsky (born 1939) had access to the most sensitive information about his country's espionage. Yet secretly he despised the Soviet system and had been spying for the West since 1966. He defected to Britain in 1985 when his Soviet masters began to suspect him.

## SECRET IDENTITY
Igor Gouzenko (1919–1982) was a cipher clerk in the Soviet Embassy in Ottawa. He did not wish to return to the Soviet Union and defected with evidence of Soviet spying. He was turned away as a crank by newspapers and government departments, but the Mounted Police believed and protected him. For this TV interview he wore a hood to keep his identity secret.

Gordievsky with his book *KGB: The Inside Story*

# Secret weapons

Espionage has a bloody past. Spies were busiest in wartime, when there was danger everywhere, and when war ended it was the job of intelligence organizations to make sure peace continued. Many wartime spies carried weapons openly, others disguised their guns and knives in often ingenious ways. With the Cold War (pp. 38–39) came greater secrecy. Both Warsaw Pact and Western powers attempted killings, and some, such as the murder of Georgi Markov, succeeded. Other schemes did not: the CIA twice tried, and failed, to kill Cuba's president Fidel Castro (pp. 42–43) with poison. The agency also considered more unusual weapons. They plotted to put deadly bacteria in Castro's cigar, and to blow him up with an exploding clam while he swam in the sea. But not all the agency's weapons would have been fatal. The strangest plot aimed to humiliate Castro. By putting special powder in the communist leader's shoes, CIA agents planned to make his distinctive beard fall out!

*Pushing the trigger near the handle fired the pellet*

**DEADLY PENCIL**
Disguised as pencils, these two weapons were used in close combat. The stabbing pencil contains a cross-shaped blade, and the propelling pencil fired a single chromium-plated bullet. Agents of Britain's SOE (pp. 32–33) used them to gain a brief advantage, so that they could seize more powerful weapons from their opponents.

*Pencil is cut away here to show knife inside*

*Gun ha... no barr... limiting accurac...*

Georgi Markov in 1978

*Shortened barrel*

Modified Webley & Scott 6.35 mm pistol

*Trigger guard*

**UMBRELLA KILLER**
The Bulgarian Georgi Markov broadcast, from the BBC in London, criticism of his country's leadership. Walking home over Waterloo Bridge one day in 1978, Markov felt a sharp pain. He looked around to see a man picking up an umbrella. Markov developed a fever and died three days later. His assassin, a Bulgarian agent, had used a specially designed umbrella to fire a tiny pellet containing a powerful poison into Markov. Ten days earlier Bulgarian agents in Paris had attacked another opponent of the country's rulers, but the victim recovered.

*Gas cylinder made umbrella work like air rifle*

*Holes in tiny pellet contained poison*

**GUN BELT**
Worn on a belt under clothing, this small World War II pistol had a very short range. To be sure of a direct hit an assassin needed to be standing right next to the target. A firing cable from the buckle passed down the sleeve of the coat that covered the gun. The great advantage was that a spy could pull the trigger without anyone seeing him or her aim or fire.

## SIMPLE SLASHERS

Not all weapons were aimed at people. These razor-sharp knives were designed to destroy vehicle tires. They were small enough to hide easily, yet with a single slash an agent could gain valuable minutes in which to make an escape. Saboteurs used the knives to immobilize a vehicle completely by slashing all the tires (including the spare).

*Knife hung from thong around neck*

*Small slasher resembles ring*

## RING REVOLVER

Concealed weapons are nothing new. The well-equipped French spy of the 19th century carried this tiny revolver attached to a ring. By revolving the chamber the agent could fire five shots. Because of its small size and firing method this design was sometimes called a squeezer pistol or palm pistol.

*Because the pistol is so small, it had a very limited range*

*The ring gun can fire five bullets*

## LETHAL GLOVE

Some weapons used by spies appear more dangerous to the person using them than to the victim. An agent firing this ingenious glove pistol had to take careful aim since there was only one bullet and that could easily take off a couple of fingers. The United States Office of Naval Intelligence produced the gun for its World War II agents.

*Barrel poked out between fingers*

*Pistol is riveted to a leather glove*

*Pressing the barrel against the victim's body fired the gun*

*Canadian maple leaf*

*Concealed blade*

*French tricolor*

*Concealed blade*

*Coin has a hidden blade*

## HEEL AND COIN BLADES

Despite their vicious appearance, knives hidden in shoe heels were not intended for attack. Instead, the concealed blades allowed agents who were tied up to cut themselves free. Spies also hid knives in low denomination coins. They hoped that their guards would let them keep the loose change in their pockets—even if the guards stole the paper currency.

## MESSY KNIVES

Wartime intelligence agencies designed these small knives so they could be hidden in a coat lapel or cuff. A captured agent could use the knife to attack guards and escape. Instructors who trained the spies warned that the results were often "messy."

# The Cold War

W~HEN WORLD WAR II ENDED~ in 1945, the future looked bleak for secret agents. In fact, a golden age of espionage was about to begin. A political boundary split Europe in two. Nicknamed the "Iron Curtain," it was actually just a line on a map. To the east lay the communist world—the Soviet Union and its allies—who wanted to create a classless society that shared everything. Nations to the west, supported by the United States, were capitalist, believing in the private ownership of property and businesses. Eastern and Western nations were deeply suspicious of each other, and their intense rivalry became known as the Cold War. Spies thrived in the atmosphere of mistrust that the Cold War created. They had plenty of work, with East and West racing each other to build the biggest bombs, and each side sending spies to discover what the other side was plotting. And because of all this activity, each side needed more counterintelligence officers at home to catch enemy agents at work. On both sides of the Iron Curtain, fear of nuclear war meant that the money for spying never ran out. Finally, in 1989, the Cold War ended and the process of reuniting Germany, which had also been split in two, began.

**HUNT THE MISSILE**
Missile bases are easy to spot on photographs from spy satellites (pp. 52–53), so the United States and the Soviet Union developed submarine-based missile launchers that could hide beneath the waves. The designers of this Trident missile claimed it would be used to hit missile bunkers. Opponents believed that cities would be the real targets.

*Distinctive mushroom-shaped cloud*

**TESTING THE BOMB**
The United States tested its atom bombs in the Nevada desert, far from the prying eyes of enemy spies. The power of these bombs to destroy civilization frightened everyone, and may have gone a long way toward ensuring that neither side in the Cold War actually used one.

*Crowds cheered as everyone with a hammer and chisel chipped at the wall*

**"KEEPING THE WORLD SAFE"**
Politicians in the Cold War believed in "mutually assured destruction" (MAD). If each side had enough bombs to destroy the other, they reasoned, neither side would dare risk war. The two "superpowers," the Soviet Union and the United States, each built huge missiles with nuclear warheads. They never launched them, and these American Titan II missiles are in storage, waiting to be converted into satellite launchers.

**THE WALL DIVIDING EUROPE**
Cold War espionage was most intense in Berlin, the capital of East Germany. Berlin was situated well inside East Germany, but a wartime treaty gave France, Britain, and the United States control of West Berlin, so the city was itself divided into East and West. To prevent refugees from escaping to the West across the new border, the East Germans divided the city of Berlin by building a wall in 1961. The wall's destruction by the people in 1989 united Germany, and symbolized the end of the Cold War.

## EUROPE DIVIDED

In the Cold War, only four European nations were neutral. Most others signed pacts vowing to defend their neighbors. The Warsaw Pact united communist countries with the Soviet Union. Capitalist countries were allied with the United States as members of the North Atlantic Treaty Organization (NATO).

Finland

Norway

Sweden

Denmark

Ireland

Netherlands

United Kingdom

Soviet Union

Belgium

East Germany

Poland

Luxembourg

West Germany

Czechoslovakia

France
(NATO member, but withdrew troops from NATO command in 1966)

Austria

Hungary

Romania

Switzerland

Portugal

Spain

Italy

Yugoslavia

Bulgaria

Albania

Greece

Turkey

## BERLIN SPY SWAP

Any captured Cold War spies could expect execution or, at best, a long spell in jail—unless their government could negotiate a prisoner exchange. Under these deals, East and West swapped captured spies. The released agents walked to freedom at one of the checkpoints along the Berlin Wall.

## SHOT DOWN

Before satellites simplified spying from above the ground, the United States sent U-2 spy planes (pp. 52–53) to photograph the other side of the Iron Curtain. The Soviet Union shot one down in 1960, and captured the CIA spy pilot, Gary Powers. He did not have to serve the 10-year sentence because the Soviets freed him in 1962 in exchange for Soviet spy Rudolph Abel.

U-2 pilot Gary Powers pictured after being shot down in 1960

Iron Curtain

Neutral countries

Other capitalist nations

Full NATO members

Other communist nations

Warsaw Pact countries

Soviet Union

*Graffiti added to remains of wall after reunification*

# Spymasters

ESPIONAGE CHIEFS HAVE enormous influence. The secrecy that surrounds all intelligence work means that, although most chiefs serve their countries wisely, those who choose not to have dangerous powers. Usually spymasters take orders from a trusted group inside a country's ruling party, but often members of that party do not know what the spies are really doing. In the past, spymasters received their orders directly from the king or queen. However, in 1519 a Venetian diplomat wrote of the English king Henry VIII's first spymaster Cardinal Wolsey that he "rules both king and the entire kingdom." In the 20th century, until the Cold War ended, secret service chiefs controlled whole Eastern European nations. J. Edgar Hoover's powers grew so great while he was the FBI chief that he was able to blackmail some of the most influential politicians in the United States. Countries are now more open about the existence of their security services, but the identity of agents in the spy networks is still a closely guarded secret.

**ROMAN SOLDIER**
General Scipio Africanus Major (236–184 BCE) was among the most clever spymasters of the Roman Empire. While attacking the Spanish city of Carthago Nova, his spies discovered that the enemy's reinforcements were 10 days' march away. As a result, the navy and army under Scipio's leadership won an easy victory.

**POWER BEHIND THE THRONE**
Cardinal Wolsey (1475–1530) became the most powerful man in England as the first head of intelligence services for King Henry VIII. Wolsey's agents opened the mail sent to diplomats from Venice and other nations. To protect their secrets, the ambassadors began to write their letters in code. Thomas Cromwell took over from Wolsey as controller.

Wolsey (left) had influence over the English king Henry VIII for many years

**INDIAN INTELLIGENCE**
Mogul ruler Akbar (1542–1605) united India. As a young king, he used fakirs (holy men) as spies. During his reign (1556–1605), Akbar extended the Indian empire, reforming the government. To do this he also relied on intelligence reports provided by *kotwal* (local officials), who had a duty to employ spies.

**INVISIBLE SPIES**
The warring princes of 12th-century Japan used *ninja* as spies and silent assassins. The ninja got their name from the Japanese word meaning "to make yourself invisible." They were trained to high standards of fitness and were masters of disguise. One warlord, Takeda Shingen, so feared them that he installed a second door in his bathroom to make escape easier.

**RUSSIAN SECRET SERVICE**
The first czar of Russia, Ivan IV (1530–1584) richly deserved his nickname "The Terrible." He ruled with the help of ruthless secret agents called the *Oprichniki*. Officially security police, the Oprichniki were really thugs who terrorized whole communities, killing and torturing without fear of punishment. They wore an emblem of a dog's head and a broom, symbolizing their powers to sniff out and sweep away treason.

*Walsingham's cipher agents forged an extra paragraph asking Mary for the plotters' names*

*The letter was written in a simple code*

## FATHER OF THE SECRET SERVICE

Francis Walsingham (about 1532–1590) did much to build up the English intelligence service. His greatest achievement was to uncover a plot to murder England's queen, Elizabeth I. Walsingham's agents intercepted coded letters between the plotters and the queen's imprisoned cousin Mary, Queen of Scots. The letters proved that Mary was involved, and she was executed in February 1587.

## A NEW BROOM SWEEPS CLEAN

For nearly half a century, J. Edgar Hoover (1895–1972) was the head of the FBI, one of the functions of which was to detect enemy spies at work in the United States. Hoover's agents also snooped on the private lives of politicians, even the president himself. By threatening to make sordid secrets public, Hoover clung to his huge power. In 1947, the CIA was formed to deal with foreign security, and the power of the FBI was curbed.

## THE RED CARDINAL

Cardinal Richelieu (1585–1642) organized the Cabinet Noir, a secret police force in France. His men spied on noble families, giving Louis XIII more power. The spies gained a reputation—every French teacher of sword-fighting was thought to be an agent.

## SPY AT THE TOP

Alfred Redl (1846–1913) was Austria's chief spycatcher. He modernized the Austrian Secret Service but ran up huge personal debts. He was blackmailed into providing vital information for Russia and accepted cash to work with them for 10 years. Redl was accused of being a traitor in 1913 and shot himself rather than stand trial.

## WOLF IN SHEEP'S CLOTHING

"The man without a face" was Markus Wolf's nickname during the Cold War. He was in charge of foreign operations for East Germany's Stasi (secret police). Wolf managed highly effective spy rings in the West. Even one of the close aides of the West German chancellor, Willy Brandt (1913–1992), had been recruited and was a Stasi spy.

# The secret services

**SPY VS SPY**
*Mad* magazine's cartoon figures made fun of secret service rivalry at the height of the Cold War.

BEHIND EVERY SPY is a vast network for gathering intelligence. Organizations like the CIA and MI6 give spies documents, money, and help and collect intelligence that the spies pass on. Intelligence networks interpret information not only from human spies, but also from a host of other sources. Satellites provide some of their data and interception of radio signals supplies more. Many of their staff do nothing but read foreign newspapers, magazines, and journals. A clever analyst can learn much from these "open sources." During World War II, Russian intelligence experts noticed the United States was hoarding silver for "scientific research" and had banned all atomic physics journals. Without putting agents' lives at risk, they guessed—correctly—that the United States was developing an atom bomb.

**BEWARE OF SPIES**
The Republic of China has a large but highly secretive intelligence network. There is a Ministry of State Security (MSS) that collects information, relying on different government organizations as well as the ordinary person in the street. In the 1970s, plaques such as this one (left) were posted all over the country to warn citizens against the activities of spies. Outside China, spies are believed to operate through the country's embassies and the New China News Agency.

*Message reads: "At all times protect (our) secrets (and) everywhere guard against spies"*

The emblem of the CIA

**GUARDIANS OF THE UNITED STATES**
The Central Intelligence Agency (CIA) has collected and analyzed foreign intelligence for the United States since 1947. It is also responsible for counterintelligence abroad. The less well-known National Security Agency, which is under the control of the US Department of Defense (DoD), is actually bigger than the CIA and handles signal intelligence—codes, ciphers, and the interception of communications. A separate organization, the United States Secret Service, has responsibility for protecting the president.

Badge of MI5, the counterintelligence agency in Britain

**THE STASI**
Until Germany's two halves were reunited in 1990, the Stasi (State Security) handled intelligence for the East. East Germans had good reason to fear these secret police. The Stasi employed more than 85,000 people and had detailed files on a third of the East German population.

*Badge worn by STASI officers who were not in uniform*

**SECURITY STAR**
Britain has twin security agencies to handle intelligence and counterintelligence at home (MI5) and abroad (MI6). In 1992, Britain was the first country to appoint a woman, Stella Rimington, as the head of a major intelligence agency. Until 1995, she was director of MI5, also called the Security Service, and originally formed in 1906. MI6 is the military name for the Secret Intelligence Service, and staff refer to its shadowy director as "C."

Map showing the
Soviet Union

Badge of the PGU,
the Soviet foreign
intelligence office
before 1991

## ISRAELIS SPYING ABROAD
Israel has developed ruthlessly efficient security and intelligence services. Formed in 1949, Mossad (the Institution for Intelligence and Special Services) is responsible for foreign espionage and taking action against the country's enemies. Shin Beth (Security and Counterespionage Service) handles internal security.

*A menorah—the symbol of Judaism*

Badge of Mossad

## SPYING FOR RUSSIA
The SVR (Foreign Intelligence Service) was created in 1991 following the collapse of the Soviet Union. It became responsible for collecting intelligence outside Russia. Counterintelligence (domestic spying) activities and all other internal intelligence activities were grouped together as the Federal Security Service (FSB). Combined, the SVR and FSB are much larger than the old KGB during the Cold War.

*Vanunu's desperate message about his kidnapping in Rome*

## MOSSAD AT WORK
Agents of Mossad are particularly skilled at undercover work in foreign countries. In 1986, when Mordechai Vanunu, a senior nuclear technician, revealed that Israel was building atom bombs, Mossad agents kidnapped him in Italy and took him back to Israel to face trial and imprisonment. While in Israeli custody, Vanunu wrote a message for the press on his hand, giving details of the kidnapping.

## TARGET PRACTICE
Despite what you see in movies and on television, the work of intelligence services rarely involves assassination. Spies want secrets, not dead bodies. During the 20th century, the Russian KGB (Committee of State Security) actively conducted multiple assassinations internationally while the CIA became famous for its fanciful but unsuccessful plans to assassinate Cuban leader Fidel Castro.

Manurhin
7.65 mm
pistol

## PROTECTING FRANCE
Like many other nations, France divides its intelligence work among several organizations. The Direction Générale de la Sécurité Extérieure (DGSE) collects foreign intelligence and organizes counterintelligence abroad. The efficient Direction de la Surveillance du Territoire (DST) is controlled by the Ministry of the Interior and handles internal security. In the early 1980s, the DST was directly responsible for the expulsion of 47 Soviet diplomats suspected of spying.

*DGSE agents abroad defend themselves with automatics like this*

# Surveillance at work

**SPIES COULD BE WATCHING YOU.** Business secrets are potentially valuable to rival companies, and to obtain those secrets, subterfuge is often used by employees or outside agencies. To steal documents, industrial spies use the tools and methods of a secret agent, and to protect the same documents from snoopers, businesses must adopt counterintelligence tactics (pp. 48–49). The devices shown here all help protect office secrets from intruders. However, all of them can also monitor employees, for the espionage threat may come from inside the company. Workplace spies can watch low-paid staff who may be bribed to sell information to rivals. The spies aim to catch disgruntled managers erasing computer disks. Even office gossip can be a target for hidden microphones: it may warn that senior staff plan to leave and set up in competition.

**ARE YOU RECEIVING ME?**
Business people can learn a lot about their clients with a tiny bug like this. A sales representative making a presentation can "accidentally" leave a bugged folder in the conference room to record a client's private conversation.

**SITTING COMFORTABLY**
As more business is done over the internet, spies realize the importance of secretly accessing a person's emails and computer files for information about their financial dealings, projects, and personal life. Robotic spy software can be emailed to a target's computer disguised as a photo, music file, or a greeting card. Once inside, the software infects the computer and sends secret copies of the user's emails and files to the spy over the internet.

*Alligator clips attach to phone wire*

**BUGGING THE WORKPLACE**
An ordinary office desk telephone is an ideal hiding place for a bug (above). It has a built-in power supply and clips to the telephone line somewhere out of site ready to pick up any conversations.

**LOUD AND CLEAR**
A sales representative who has planted a bug is able to eavesdrop on his client from a car parked outside. By pulling up the radio antenna, he can pick up the signal and listen to any discussion of the sales pitch. The following day, the sales rep can return to negotiations, able to use the information to change strategy, and ready to bargain.

## PINHOLE PEEPER
More than one in every 10 American companies uses video cameras to spy on its employees. Concealing the cameras is simple: the smallest have lenses that are much smaller than a match head.

## CAUGHT ON CAMERA
FBI agents used a hidden video camera in 1979 to collect evidence in a corruption case that they nicknamed "ABSCAM." The video (above) proved that members of the US Congress were taking bribes. Seven members of Congress were convicted and went to prison.

## INFINITY RECEIVER
Most office bugs have a limited range but infinity receivers use the telephone lines to allow eavesdropping from anywhere in the world that there is a telephone. The "spy" must first install the device, usually attached to the telephone line. The bug does not operate until the spy dials the number of the bugged telephone, followed by a specially selected key on a touch-tone telephone. The bug detects the tone and stops the target phone from ringing. Then it allows the spy to hear a conversation in the room, using the telephone mouthpiece as a microphone. With the infinity receiver, it is possible for someone in Sydney, Australia, for example, to eavesdrop on conversations in Washington, DC.

*USB connector plugs into computer*

## THANKS FOR THE MEMORIES
A USB flash stick is a memory storage device with a universal connector that works on almost any computer. About the size of your thumb, it is easily hidden and can be used by a spy to secretly copy hundreds of thousands of pages of documents stored inside a computer network. Most intelligence services have removed the USB connectors from their computers to prevent theft of their documents.

## BUG IN A PLUG
Disguised as a wall socket, a bug is impossible to detect without taking the socket apart or using special equipment. The socket functions normally and also supplies the bug with power. Some devices work like baby alarms, using the power cables—instead of radio waves—to transmit signals. The spy monitors any conversations with a suitable receiver plugged into any other socket on the same circuit.

## ROBOTIC EYES
Although usually associated with street surveillance, some offices have monitoring rooms where security officers use closed circuit television cameras (CCTV) to watch and protect employees as well as reporting suspicious activity. Cameras are connected to large digital storage devices and the internet. If a spy can learn the company's secret computer password he can monitor activities from anywhere in the world.

# Industrial espionage

GOVERNMENTS AND POLITICIANS are not the only targets of espionage. Businesses also have secrets that industrial spies try to steal or copy. This kind of espionage is rapidly expanding, but it is hardly new. The silk industry was an early victim. Until the 6th century, only the Chinese knew how to make this luxurious cloth. Then the Byzantine emperor Justinian I (483–565) used espionage to steal the secret of its production. He encouraged two monks to smuggle silkworms out of China in hollow canes. Industrial spying is more sophisticated today, but governments still encourage it if their nation benefits. In 1989, the French Department of Commerce planned to steal trade secrets from American and British companies. The spying became public when an informer mailed their "shopping list" to the CIA. Usually, though, it is businesses that use industrial espionage against their competitors. Successful spies find design details, lists of suppliers and buyers. Even advance knowledge of a price list can help squeeze a competitor out of business.

## SPYING ON THE COMPETITION

One of the most common forms of industrial espionage is for trusted employees to quit and join a competitor—taking secrets with them. General Motors (GM) suspected Jose Ignacio Lopez do Arriortua of doing this when he left to join rival Volkswagen. GM claimed that de Arriortua and other executives left GM with thousands of photographs and plans of the Opel Vectra that was then secret. There have been similar scandals in Formula 1 racing car design. In 2007 McLaren was fined for possessing confidential Ferrari information.

*Computer-aided designs of new cars are fiercely protected from industrial espionage*

General Motors' Opel Vectra

*In the US, billions of dollars are lost each year through audio, software, and DVD piracy*

*Long before they emerge on the catwalk, designs of evening dresses are the target of spies*

## THE ENTERTAINMENT INDUSTRY

Piracy (illegal copying) and industrial espionage cut the profits made by people in the world of entertainment. From a single original, pirates can make millions of CDs or DVDs. Security at recording and film studios must be intense to make sure that master tapes are protected until the scheduled release date. Despite these precautions, industrial spies occasionally succeed in smuggling out a recording: pirates made thousands of illegal copies of the James Bond film *Casino Royale* and distributed them throughout Asia before the film's London première.

*To keep the shape of a new car secret, it can be disguised by fitting new parts in old car bodies when being road-tested*

*Revolutionary disk braking systems may interest rival car manufacturers*

## COSTUME DRAMA

Theft of ideas and designs in the fashion industry is big business. It is easy to claim and often difficult to prove. Cutters and other workers in the garment trade might copy patterns and sell them to another designer. It is also possible to re-create designs from sketches or photographs taken at designer dress shows.

## INDUSTRIAL DIAMONDS

An industrial spy at General Electric earned more than $1 million for passing secrets of synthetic diamond manufacture to a South Korean company. By stealing the knowledge they needed to build the plant, the Koreans avoided paying license fees for the technology, and in addition saved the enormous expense of funding a research and development program. General Electric discovered the espionage in 1992.

*Tiny synthetic diamonds in drill's tip help it cut faster*

## COMPUTER SPYING

In 1981, the FBI caught a computer engineer, Kenji Hayashi, with secret details of IBM computer disk drive technology. His employers, Japan's Hitachi corporation, gave him more than half a million dollars that he used to bribe IBM staff. After his arrest and trial, Hitachi had to pay IBM 60 times this sum in compensation.

# Counterintelligence

IN THE PAST, bugging equipment was often simple, and wires from hidden microphones sometimes led directly to eavesdropping spies. Today, finding bugs and wiretaps—and the spies who use them—is harder, especially as much of it is conducted over the internet. It is the job of counterintelligence agencies to track them down. However, detection of spies does not always lead to their capture—sometimes an enemy spy is more valuable if allowed to carry on as normal. Working spies can provide a counterintelligence agency with useful information, especially if they do not know they are being watched. A spy's activities can give away secrets about spying techniques and equipment. These details can be used to help trap other spies. Counterintelligence services also use unmasked spies to feed false information to their enemies. Sometimes, by confronting spies with evidence of their guilt, a counterintelligence agency can force the spies to work against their original masters as double agents.

**SOMEONE IS WATCHING YOU**
Counterespionage agencies use many of the same tools as the spies themselves. This 19th-century cartoon makes fun of the craze for hidden cameras among spies and counterspies alike.

**KEEPING CALLS SECRET**
During the Cold War, portable scramblers were sometimes used to keep telephone calls private. A typical scrambler breaks up speech into short segments, then rearranges these into an apparently random order for transmission down the telephone line. The receiving scrambler reverses the process. The people talking hear each other perfectly, but a spy who taps the line will hear nothing but "gray noise" (a meaningless jumble of sound). Modern digital scramblers utilize software with built-in encryption to protect conversations sent over the internet against eavesdropping.

Cold war scrambler attached to telephone

**SETTING THE CODE**
A caller uses a row of tiny switches to set their scrambler to the same prearranged code as the receiving scrambler.

**COUNTERSPY'S TOOLKIT**
When checking for bugs, the counterspy uses screwdrivers and other basic tools to undo plug casings and look behind light sockets and other likely places. A visual inspection can reveal damage left when a bug was installed. And by comparing every cable with a wiring diagram a counterspy can confirm whether there are cables linking microphones to a distant transmitter.

*Rising tone in headphones indicates presence of a bug*

*Handle is removable to aid search of cramped spaces*

*Reducing power output helps pinpoint hidden bugs*

*Probe detects bugs even when they are not transmitting*

**A NEW BROOM**
This device is used by a counterintelligence officer to quickly sweep (check) a room for bugs. The probe gives off a radio signal, which energizes semiconductor devices, such as transistors or integrated circuits. This creates a tell-tale signal that the "broom" detects. Innocent electronic devices such as telephones will activate the detector, but once these are taken into account, any remaining signals probably come from a concealed bug.

**Strength of signal**

55

0

*Peaks indicate where there is a bug*

Frequency

20 MHz

12 MHz

**WHICH ROOM IS BUGGED?**
By displaying many scans from a tuned receiver in three-dimensional form, a room that contains a bug is revealed. The graph plots signal strength and frequency in megahertz (MHz) for each room of a building.

*High peak indicates strong signal*

*This trace indicates the presence of a bug*

*Portable computer visually interprets information from Scanlock receiver*

*Antenna picks up broadcast signals*

**LOOKING AROUND CORNERS**
Many offices have large spaces under the floor, above the ceiling and within the walls. These cavities are big enough to hide sophisticated and bulky monitoring equipment. To check such hiding places, countersurveillance staff use small mirrors and tiny lights. Flexible goosenecks on the handles allow the searcher to insert the mirror deep inside inaccessible places.

*Flexible goose-neck*

*Tiny mirror reaches in smallest holes*

*Batteries in the handle power lamps*

*Device makes high-pitched sound if it detects a bug*

**SCANLOCK DETECTOR**
Detecting cheap bugs is easy: play music in the suspect room, then use a radio receiver to scan commonly used frequencies until you hear the music. More sophisticated bugs avoid such countermeasures by broadcasting on unusual frequencies, by hopping between frequencies, or by scrambling their signals. This Scanlock wide-coverage tuned receiver picks up these "smart" bugs by scanning all the transmission frequencies within minutes.

*Signal strength meter leads operator to bug*

**BUGS ON DISPLAY**
Connecting the Scanlock receiver to a portable computer displays its output in visual form. The jagged lines give a skilled operator much more information about radio signals in the surrounding area. Higher peaks indicate stronger signals. Each trace forms a picture of radio signal activity at one particular time. If a bug then switches on, its signal will change the shape of a later trace.

**PINPOINTING A BUG**
Once counterespionage agents are sure a room is bugged, they can use a lightweight signal-strength meter to track it down. These handheld devices require no tuning and show a stronger signal the closer they are to the source.

# Spy-catching

LOCATING AND IDENTIFYING SPIES is rarely easy—unless a mole or defector betrays them. Suspicious radio signals can sometimes allow counterintelligence agents to pinpoint a hidden transmitter. By tapping telephones and secretly opening mail a counterspy can find a few, and patient surveillance catches many more. Careless spies can give themselves, and others, away when collecting intelligence. For example, following a suspected spy sometimes leads to the discovery of other unknown agents. Once they are caught they must be "neutralized"—this means exposing them so they cannot work secretly, expelling them to their home countries, or prosecuting and imprisoning them. In some countries neutralization can have a more sinister meaning—an unfair trial and a death sentence.

**BLEEPS TRACE MISSILE SECRETS**
A tip-off by a defector alerted Britain's MI5 to spy Frank Bossard (born 1912). They caught him by attaching a transmitter to the files he "borrowed" from his Air Ministry office. The beacon's radio bleeps led MI5 officers to where the spy was copying the documents.

*Probe fits through slit at top of envelope and jaws grip the letter*

**SUSPICIOUS SPY-CATCHER**
As counterintelligence chief of the CIA, James Jesus Angleton (1917–1987) hunted spies for two decades. He trusted nobody and suspected every defector of being a KGB double agent. He found few moles, however, and his intense suspicion slowed the agency's work. By ordering illegal mail interceptions he damaged his reputation and was fired in 1974.

*Winding handle rolls letter into tight coil*

*Applying invisible crayon sticks powder to a surface*

*By pulling handle agent pulls out letter*

*The Rosenbergs are taken from court after being convicted*

**FLAPS AND SEALS**
Counterespionage agents use tools like this to open letters, read them, and replace them without tearing the envelope. This skill, known as "flaps and seals," allows them to monitor letters addressed to a spy. Letters mailed by the spy, however, are much more difficult to intercept.

**ROUGH JUSTICE**
Harsh punishment of spies has sometimes aroused strong emotions. Julius and Ethel Rosenberg were caught giving secrets to the Soviet Union. They were the first American spies sentenced to death during peacetime and many people begged for mercy for them. Despite this, they were convicted for their espionage during World War II, condemned, and finally died in the electric chair in 1953.

### CAUGHT IN THE ACT
Video surveillance can catch a spy at work, but checking tapes from many cameras is very time-consuming. New digital cameras linked to surveillance software (see pp. 44–45) can recognize faces and identify known spies in a crowd of people even if they are disguised. Once spotted, the computers will automatically track and record the spy's movements while alerting security officers.

*Surveillance cameras can be used to track a suspect's movements*

*MERSH agent's identity card*

*Ultraviolet light shows up anti-bugging seals*

### "DEATH TO SPIES"
The Soviet counterespionage organization Smert Shpionam (roughly translated as "death to spies") was responsible for military security, and for catching spies within the country's intelligence services. The agency soon acquired the nickname "SMERSH."

### CHECKING SEALS
After a bugging sweep counterintelligence agents use seals to secure "clean" areas. An ultraviolet lamp is used to show up the antibugging stickers to check they are not broken.

### RED-HANDED
By dusting secret files with these special powders (left), counterintelligence agents can catch a spy who handles the material. Powder sticking to the spy's hands glows under light from sources such as the ultraviolet lantern (above right).

*RFID chip transmits radio waves over a range of more than 300 ft (90 m)*

### CHIPS WITH EVERYTHING
RFID (Radio-Frequency Identification) chips only slightly larger than the period at the end of this sentence are called "taggants" and can be attached to a person's clothing, shoes, or even a passport or ID card and used to track his movements secretly. Security services, such as Britain's MI5, use RFID chips in London to monitor foreign spies posing as diplomats.

*Powder is invisible in normal light when sprinkled on files*

# Spying without spies

THE WORK OF REAL LIVE SPIES—or HUMINT (human intelligence)—is both costly and slow, and if a spy is discovered this could embarrass politicians. Fortunately, there are some alternatives. Technical intelligence-gathering uses remote sensors which can do the spy's work from a distance. COMINT (communications intelligence); SIGINT (signals); ELINT (electronic), and IMINT (imagery) all provide valuable knowledge. Perhaps the most important is IMINT, which is the gathering of pictures from cameras and radar in spy aircraft and satellites. These provide amazing views of objects on the ground—some can even distinguish between civilians and soldiers. Just as satellites improve a spy's distant vision, technical intelligence far below makes other senses keener. Seabed hydrophones track the sound of enemy submarines and, like sensitive fingertips, seismographs detect the vibrations caused by atomic tests.

**SPY PLANES WITHOUT PILOTS**
*Darkstar* is a drone, or uncrewed aerial vehicle (UAV), developed in the United States. UAVs can take detailed air photographs of heavily defended enemy territory without risking a pilot's life.

**SPY SATELLITE LAUNCH**
Older spy satellites used film because the pictures produced were sharper than video. The film fell to Earth in a capsule for collection and processing. Such spy satellites are still secret. This Soviet launch carries a civilian version into orbit.

Russian KFA satellite on ground after re entry

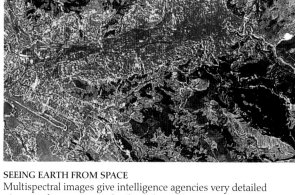

**SEEING EARTH FROM SPACE**
Multispectral images give intelligence agencies very detailed pictures of war zones and military bases, but they do not show the landscape in true colors. In this image of Sarajevo in former Yugoslavia, electronic processing has made buildings stand out in pink. With greater enlargement, pictures can record objects as small as a truck.

*Sensors behind colored windows view targets in both visible light and infrared*

*Engines power the* Blackbird *forward three times faster than the speed of sound*

**EYES IN THE SKIES**
American Keyhole 12 spy satellites can see objects as small as a grapefruit from a distance of 250 miles (400 km). No nation releases pictures of its spy satellites. However, this Earth observation satellite, which is used for map-making, is built in the same way. Radar imaging allows spy satellites to look straight through cloud cover and infrared sensors can even pick out heat shadows left by a missile launch. Multispectral cameras in the satellite make it possible to distinguish between real trees and camouflage.

**U-2 SPY PLANE**
The CIA welcomed this high-flying spy plane as a triumph when it first flew in 1955 because they believed it was more accurate and dependable, and could collect information faster, than any agent on the ground. The U-2 could cruise well above 65,000 ft (20,000 m), but this proved not high enough when a Soviet missile shot one down in 1960. The pilot was captured (pp. 38–39).

*Aircraft is very light in weight to increase range*

*Cockpit is not pressurized: pilot breathes pure oxygen from a helmet*

*Explosion was equivalent to an earthquake with a magnitude of 6.2 on the Richter scale*

ground up

**TRACING THE BIG BANGS**
Seismographs make vibrations in Earth's crust visible as a trace on paper. Geologists normally use them to monitor earthquakes, but the instruments can also register underground nuclear tests on the other side of the world. In September 1949, United States intelligence analysts got their first firm evidence that the Soviet Union had developed the atom bomb from a trace like this one.

*Trace shows activity at the Soviet Union's Kazakhstan test site in central Asia*

**TAKING A CLOSE LOOK**
This is a unique photograph taken in 1984 of a Soviet aircraft carrier under construction in a Black Sea shipyard. The picture shows the ship's hull being built in two separate sections. Computer enhancement and color have improved the quality of the picture.

*Black paint is needed to dissipate heat, because friction with the atmosphere warms the plane to 800°F (427°C)*

**BLACKBIRD WITH SHARP EYES**
The *Blackbird* reconnaissance plane was built to replace the U-2. Though designed in 1959, the two-seater still flies higher and faster than any other aircraft. It can cross the Atlantic in less than two hours and photograph a country the size of Mexico in 13 hours. Lockheed developed the U-2, the *Blackbird*, and *Darkstar* at a top-secret plant in Burbank, California, known as the "Skunk Works," later moving to Palmdale, California. *Blackbirds* collected intelligence for more than 20 years during the Cold War, but were mothballed (taken out of service) to save money in 1990. Five years later, the US Air Force reconditioned several of them, and once more began training aircrew to fly surveillance missions.

**SKY HIGH EYE**
Satellite data helps environmentalists monitor climate change and loss of habitat because of human activity or natural disaster. Spy satellites take the sharpest pictures, but until recently these have been kept secret. Now the US makes its images available to the general public. They will give researchers a clearer picture of how Earth has changed over the last 40 years.

# Spying today

SPIES THRIVED IN THE COLD WAR. While it lasted, the United States and the Soviet Union feared each other's bombs and missiles and needed intelligence agencies to help keep the peace. Initially, when the Cold War ended in the late 1980s, many spies lost their jobs. Intelligence agencies had to adapt quickly. They looked for new uses for their spy technology and some formed alliances with the scientific community. Technology developed for global surveillance was adapted for use in other areas. Besides tracking submarines, America's secret hydrophone network listened in to the sound of whales. Today, intelligence services still use the hydrophones, along with advanced satellites to keep track of enemy submarines. Earth observing satellites, once reserved for intelligence agencies, are now run by private companies. Intelligence agencies found that their skills in catching spies were just as useful in identifying terrorists. Intelligence officers who had trailed Cold War traitors now followed Colombian drug barons. However, the relative quiet period for intelligence services that came in the immediate aftermath of the Cold War, in the early 1990s, gradually abated. Now the Russian intelligence service, as well as the CIA, is much larger than it was during the Cold War.

**DRUGS ON THE STREET**
Intelligence agencies can collect information about the production and the smuggling of narcotics. However, the war on drugs does not end when shipments reach their destination. Kits like these (left) help agents catch drug dealers. The sprays quickly identify drugs wherever they are, avoiding the cost and delay of laboratory analysis.

**EVERCHANGING ROLE**
However much the world changes, there will always be a role for secret agents. The danger of war in Eastern Europe has largely disappeared only to be replaced by war and political instability in the Middle East. US Secret Service agents also have an important role to play guarding the president.

*US Secret Service man protects President Bush at an antidrug summit*

**DRUGS SNOOPER**
The war against drugs increasingly relies on American satellites that were once used to police nuclear weapon treaties. High above Colombia, a "spy in the sky" can identify jungle landing strips, drug laboratories and storage areas. Using information gathered by satellite pictures, Colombian soldiers swoop on the bases with helicopters and ground troops. They have seized vast amounts of cocaine in single raids.

*Shoulder bag conceals a machine-gun*

Fuel rod contains
pellets of nuclear
material

### FUELING FEAR

Terrorists need 16 lb (7 kg) of plutonium from a nuclear power
plant to build a bomb, and workers in Russia's crumbling nuclear
industry are happy to sell it. Intelligence services across the world
cooperate in tracing this stolen plutonium and uranium.

*Plutonium sealed
inside is highly
poisonous, but
radiation it emits
is not a danger to
bomb-makers*

### SHINING PATH

Behind bars, Abimael
Guzman no longer leads
the Shining Path
guerrilla movement that
terrorized Peru for more
than 20 years, killing
25,000 people. Police
used spy tactics to catch
him in 1992, first
collecting intelligence,
and then staking out his
apartment with agents
in disguise.

### ORGANIZED CRIME

In the United States, the
FBI tracks spies and fights
organized crime gangs such
as the Mafia and Chinese
Triads. Counterintelligence
and security organizations,
such as MI5 in Britain, have
only recently joined the
police in the fight.

*Gamblers gather at the
headquarters of New
York's Hung Mon
Association, which
has direct links with
Triad gangs*

### SPY IN THE SKY

Satellites with powerful digital cameras are able to photograph
objects as small as 3 in (75 mm) from space and transmit instant
pictures back to intelligence services. Events can be analyzed as they
are happening to provide current information to military and
national leadership, by departments such as the National
Reconnaissance Office (NRO). But who has access to that
information? In 2001, former NRO employee Brian Regan contacted
the Iraqi government just before the invasion and offered to sell
US satellite secrets revealing US knowledge of the locations of
Iraqi weapons.

*Receiving antenna collects
incoming radio signal*

*Transmitting antenna
can direct signal back
to multiple
destinations*

# Spying and you

YOU ARE UNDER SURVEILLANCE! Every day, cameras capture you walking along the street and the journeys you make in your car. Your cell phone calls and the sites you surf on the internet are logged by communications providers, and your shopping purchases are recorded by supermarkets and stores. And it's not just you—the same goes for every other member of the public. Governments around the world are also busy compiling databases on their populations, from people's medical records and identifying features to details of their financial dealings. Such monitoring helps to make our countries and neighborhoods more secure, our health services more efficient, and our leisure time more rewarding—but it also comes with the potential for misuse.

**CAUGHT ON CAMERA**
For many people, CCTV proved its worth in the aftermath of the terrorist bombing in London on July 7, 2005. CCTV footage showed the bombers on their way to the capital on the morning of the attack, and also on a reconnaissance trip to London nine days before the blasts (above). The footage enabled the police to identify the bombers within hours of the attack.

*Cameras can be remotely controlled to pan, tilt, and zoom in for a closer view of targets*

*Operator can select a camera and use it to investigate anything that seems "unusual"*

**CCTV MONITORING CENTER**
London contains more CCTV cameras (*see* p. 45) per square mile than any other city. Police officers sit in front of vast arrays of television monitors connected to public and private surveillance cameras throughout the London area. The CCTV cameras are linked to large-capacity digital storage drives, where the images are labeled with a date/time stamp and archived for future study. In some CCTV systems, an operator can "mark" a suspicious individual, who is then tracked automatically from camera to camera. Civil liberties groups complain that people should be able to go about their daily lives without being under constant surveillance, but the authorities argue that CCTV makes criminals beware and the streets safer.

**EYES AND EARS OF THE POLICE**
Many roads and streets are under constant watch by CCTV cameras. Some cameras record traffic flow and read car license plates, others monitor pedestrians. Multiple microphones mounted on CCTV towers can also listen for problems such as gunshots. The directions from which sounds reach the microphones are used to calculate the position of the shot and guide police to the scene.

### TODDLER TRACKERS

Toylike beacons, such as the Giggle Bug Toddler Tracker® shown here, can be used by parents to prevent their toddlers from getting lost. Containing an RFID tag, the tracker makes a bleeping sound when a parent presses the button on the handheld fob, revealing the child's location within a 100-ft (30-m) radius. Similar devices using Global Positioning System (GPS) chips allow companies to track their laptop computers and locate key employees as they travel around. Such technologies could also be used to monitor a person's movements without their knowledge.

*Pressing the fob reveals whereabouts of child*

Giggle Bug Toddler Tracker®

*Ladybug tag clips on to child's clothes*

*Computer scanner records iris pattern*

Touch-screen shopping cart for RFID-tagged goods

### ̇E KNOW WHAT YOU BUY...

̇stead of marking products with bar codes, some stores use ̇ID tags (*see* p. 51). When placed in a shopping cart, the ̇ on the product is detected by an onboard receiver. RFID ̇rchases are logged by the store's database and used to order ̇w stock. The data can also be used to analyze people's ̇ending habits. There are concerns that the tags may one day ̇ able to be traced to the customer's home, which some people ̇ as a threat to their privacy. Stores dismiss these worries, ̇ying that the tags would be deactivated at the store's exit.

### IRIS SCANNING

Biometric data such as fingerprints, DNA samples, and iris scans can be used to identify people—trusted individuals, criminals, and terrorists alike. Each person has unique patterns of blood vessels on their irises (the colored rings around the eyes' black pupils). An iris scanner analyzes these patterns and compares them to those on a database to see if there are any matches. In theory, biometric data could also be used by the state to keep tabs on civilians it considers politically troublesome.

### ̇NLINE PERILS

̇ery time you visit a website, you unknowingly leave ̇ell-tale sign known as a "cookie." These details can ̇ used to compile data on your internet activity. ̇ownloading files that have not been checked for ̇ruses may allow a hacker to secretly access private ̇formation on your hard drive, and even remotely ̇n on your web cam without your knowledge. Social ̇tworking sites like Facebook and MySpace allow ̇u to link with like-minded people anywhere. But be ̇reful—not everyone is truthful, and your new online ̇uddy" might be predator lurking in disguise.

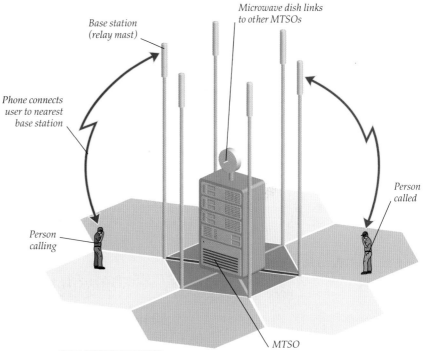

*Microwave dish links to other MTSOs*

*Base station (relay mast)*

*Phone connects user to nearest base station*

*Person calling*

*Person called*

MTSO

### CELL PHONE TRACING

A cell phone company divides the area it serves into a grid of hexagonal "cells." Each base station (relay mast) is located at the point where three cells meet. Two people talking on the phone are each connected to their nearest base station. The base stations are linked via an MTSO (Mobile Telephone Switching Office). The phone company's log shows which base stations took part in the call and their relative signal strengths. This information can be used by emergency services and police to calculate a user's position to within 125 ft (38 m).

# Famous spies

THE MOST SUCCESSFUL SPIES do not become famous. As soon as their work is complete, they disappear into the shadows. Wartime spies are the exception to this. When the fighting ends, they tell their stories and sometimes earn high honors. As a reward for her spying, and for enduring torture and imprisonment, Odette Sansom received one of Britain's most important medals, the George Cross. Not everybody believed that she deserved it. Yvonne Cormeau (pp. 32–33) complained that other SOE agents got a lesser award because "we haven't been caught." Of course, all spies try to avoid capture, but if it happens, fame can follow quickly. Their captors are eager to put the spies' crimes on show. Spy trials often disappoint newspaper readers who follow them—in a real spy's life glamour is rare, and the routine boring.

However, a few spies do live lives as exciting as any novel. Some actually turn into fictional characters: Ian Fleming based James Bond on the spy Dusko Popov.

Sean Connery as Bond in the film of *Dr. No*

**WILL THE REAL SPY STAND UP?**
Fictional James Bond in the first Bond film, 1962 (top) and real spy Dusko Popov (above with his wife) both enjoyed gambling and the company of beautiful women. Bond's creator, Ian Fleming (pp. 60–61), met Popov in 1941 when Fleming was a British naval intelligence officer.

*For her stage act, Mata Hari wore elaborate costumes and headdresses, but often danced naked as well*

*Mata Hari falsely claimed to be the daughter of a temple dancer and that she had been dedicated to the god Shiva*

**FAILED SPY**
As Mata Hari, exotic dancer Margaretha Macleod (1876–1917) entertained German officers in France during World War I. Although she became one of the most famous names in the history of espionage, she was not very good at spying. She was recruited by the German Secret Service, but they did not entirely trust her, and she offered her services to the Allies. Germany finally betrayed her to France and on October 15, 1917, she was executed by a French firing squad.

**CODENAME "WHITE RABBIT"**
Welsh Royal Air Force officer "Tommy" Yeo-Thomas became famous after his arrest and torture by the Gestapo, the German secret police, during World War II. He had been working for the SOE (pp. 32–33), organizing the French resistance to German troops occupying France. He was betrayed and captured outside a subway station in Paris. Tortured by the Gestapo, he was imprisoned but escaped from the death camp at Buchenwald in Germany.

*Forged papers gave "White Rabbit" cover stories on his visits to France*

Donald Maclean (1913–1983) passed atom bomb secrets to Moscow

Guy Burgess (1911–1963) attracted attention with his drunken violence

Kim Philby (1912–1988) warned Maclean and Burgess when to flee

Anthony Blunt (1907–1983) helped the others escape to the Soviet Union

*Odette Sansom was the first woman to win the George Cross*

Odette Sansom with the dolls in 1954

*Dolls entirely handsewn*

*Ski sticks made from card and silver foil*

## WARTIME HEROINE

During World War II, Odette Sansom (1912–1995) worked as "Céline," an agent for the Allied Special Operations Executive (SOE). She helped organize resistance groups in southern France. Betrayed by a double agent in 1943, Odette was captured and taken to Fresnes Prison near Paris, where she was horribly tortured. After Fresnes, she was transferred to a prison in Germany and then to a concentration camp. Making these dolls for the nephew and niece of a German Catholic priest helped her pass the long hours of captivity. She was finally freed by the Allies in May 1945. The cruelty of her ordeal and the valor with which she faced it have made her a legendary wartime spy.

## THE CAMBRIDGE FIVE

Four of the 20th century's most notorious spies met at Cambridge University, England. While working for Britain's Foreign Office, Guy Burgess and Donald Maclean leaked secrets to Moscow, fleeing there in 1951 when MI5 began to suspect them. When the "third man" Kim Philby (pp. 34–35) joined them in 1961, a "fourth man," Anthony Blunt, secretly admitted to spying. In return for his confession, Blunt kept his job as Surveyor of the Queen's Pictures until he retired. However, by 1979, his name had become public knowledge and, later, a "fifth man," John Cairncross, was revealed.

## SHOW TRIAL VICTIM

Soviet military intelligence officer Oleg Penkowsky (1919–1963) contacted Western intelligence agencies in 1960. He believed he could prevent war by telling the West about Soviet nuclear missiles. The secrets he provided gave the United States a real advantage in the Cold War. The KGB caught Penkowsky and he was given a show trial at which he "confessed." He was sentenced to death and reportedly executed in 1963.

59

# Spies in fiction

*Michael Caine played Harry Palmer in the 1965 film version of* The Ipcress File

ESPIONAGE HAS ALL THE INGREDIENTS for an exciting storybook or movie: suspense, action, intrigue, and natural drama. American author James Fenimore Cooper (1789–1851) helped establish the spy story with his book *The Spy* in 1851, but spy novels have only really become popular in the last 50 years. Some of the most successful authors were themselves spies. Ian Fleming worked for British naval intelligence during World War II. John Le Carré drew on his experience of MI5 and MI6 to create a more authentic picture of the secret agent's world. Hollywood turned the books of both authors and many more into successful movies, but the books and films did not always impress real spies. Allen Dulles, once head of the CIA, wrote that "spy heroes… rarely exist in real life." This did not stop the CIA from using spy films to train agents on the finer points and pitfalls of their trade.

### ANTI-HERO
In *The Ipcress File*, writer Len Deighton created a spy hero who shared only his nationality with James Bond. The story of the Cockney petty criminal turned reluctant spy was Deighton's hugely successful first book.

*Bond uses a piton gun to fire rope during a spectacular bungee jump in the opening sequence*

*Grappling hook at end of rope*

### AUTHOR MEETS SPY
Frederick Forsyth (left) based his book *The Odessa File* on the exploits of the German "Champagne Spy" Wolfgang Lotz (right). Lotz crippled the Egyptian missile program, helping Israel win the Six Day War against Egypt in 1967.

*Lotz's high lifestyle earned him his nickname of "the Champagne Spy."*

### SPY HIT LIST
British spies may not be the world's best, but the country's espionage writers top the best-seller lists. In the 1960s, their anti-Communist message alarmed the KGB. The Soviets hit back with *The Zakhov Mission*, in which a communist hero defeats 007. It could not compete with the success of Fleming's originals, which have been translated all over the world.

### FICTIONAL EVIL LADY
"We are enveloped in a network of spies," cries D'Artagnan, the young hero who helps the three musketeers in the famous adventure story written by Alexander Dumas (1802–1870). Milady (right) is the most deadly of the spies who are employed by Cardinal Richelieu (pp. 40–41) to try and discredit the Queen of France.

### INDIAN ROPE TRICK

High-tech gadgetry is as much the star in a Bond film as 007 himself. In the Bond books, Ian Fleming based these devices on genuine inventions supplied by people such as Charles Fraser-Smith to World War II agents (pp. 10–11).

*Buckle conceals 75-ft (27-m) long fine rope that can bear Bond's weight*

Bond's belt worn in the film *Goldeneye*

*Telescopic sights*

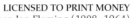

### TIME TOOL

Watches play a leading role in many of the Bond films. In *Goldeneye*, a laser built into Bond's watch helps him cut his way out of difficult situations. The KGB studied James Bond films in order to develop their own spy technology.

James Bond's piton gun from the film *GoldenEye*

*Piton gun contains laser that Bond uses to cut open the roof of a Russian chemical plant*

### LICENSED TO PRINT MONEY

When Ian Fleming (1908–1964) created the character of James Bond, he was aiming to write the spy story "to end all spy stories." He succeeded. The 14 Bond books sold more than 18 million copies.

*In GoldenEye, the seventeenth James Bond film, Pierce Brosnan plays the sophisticated British spy*

*Bond destroyed the chemical plant using a magnetic mine*

*The true-to-life bugging toolkit includes a lock-pick gun*

### BUGGED BATHROOM

In the film *The Conversation*, a bugging expert (played by Gene Hackman) is drawn into a terrifying world of deception and murder. As nerve-racking as any political spy story, the film is a rare and authentic glimpse of industrial espionage at work.

# Rogues' gallery of spies

Some spies work for decades without discovery, but if a spy is uncovered and put on trial, it often makes headlines and he or she becomes a figure of public hate. Occasionally, spies manage to escape from prison or the clutches of counterintelligence officers and flee to the country for which they spied. There they are celebrated as daring adventurers, but in the country where they spied they remain not just rogues but vile traitors who put the nation's security, business, and people at risk.

### ABEL, RUDOLPH
A KGB mole (*see* p. 9), Abel was the KGB's chief agent in the US until he was arrested in 1957. He was swapped in 1962 for US pilot Gary Powers, who had been shot down over the Soviet Union in 1960. Abel was given a hero's welcome in Moscow and spent the rest of his life teaching KGB trainees.

### AGEE, PHILIP
Codenamed "Pont," Agee was a CIA officer who worked covertly for Cuban intelligence and the KGB. He revealed the names of 2,000 undercover CIA officers, including Richard Welch, the CIA chief in Greece. This led to the murder of Welch outside his home. Agee died in Cuba in 2008.

### BARNETT, DAVID H.
In 1976, former-CIA-officer Barnett began selling secrets to the KGB to pay off debts, including details of HA/BRINK, a CIA operation that collected information on weaponry given by the Soviets to Indonesia. Barnett also betrayed the identities of more than 30 CIA officers.

### BELL, WILLIAM H.
William Bell worked on radar at the Hughes Aircraft Corporation in California. Faced with financial difficulties, he agreed to sell radar secrets to Marian Zacharski, a Polish intelligence officer. In 1981, Bell was confronted by FBI agents. He confessed and helped the FBI to catch Zacharski.

### BLAKE, GEORGE
While a senior intelligence officer for MI6, George Blake was also spying secretly for the KGB because he believed in the principles of Communism. Blake was betrayed by a Polish defector in 1961. He escaped from Wormwood Scrubs Prison, London, in 1966, and eventually made his way to Moscow, where he took up residence.

*Rudolph Abel*

*George Blake*

### BOYCE, CHRISTOPHER J.
A US defense industry employee, Boyce and his friend Andrew Doulton Lee were arrested in 1977 for selling satellite secrets to the Soviets, which they passed to KGB officers in Mexico. Boyce later escaped from prison, but was recaptured after 19 months on the run.

### CARNEY, JEFFREY M.
Carney, a US Air Force intelligence specialist, spied for the East German HVA (foreign intelligence service) while stationed in West Germany. He continued spying on his return to the US, but in 1985 defected to East Germany. Carney was arrested by US counterintelligence officers two years after the collapse of the East German state.

### COHEN, ELI
This Egyptian-born linguist was recruited by Israeli intelligence to infiltrate Syria's ruling Baath Party. He supplied Israel with information about the Syrian military and its fortifications on the strategically important Golan Heights. Cohen was arrested in 1965 and executed.

### CONRAD, CLYDE L.
A retired US Army sergeant, Conrad was arrested in West Germany in 1988 for passing classified material to Hungarian intelligence, including NATO plans for the defense of Europe. He is thought to have been aided by at least a dozen other army personnel—one of the biggest spy rings since World War II.

### GIMPEL, ERIC
In 1944, during World War II, a German submarine landed Gimpel and fellow German spy William Colepaugh on a beach in Maine. The spies went to New York, where they lived the high life using the money intended for their espionage. Colepaugh turned himself in to the FBI and helped them to catch Gimpel.

### HAMBLETON, HUGH
In 1956, Hambleton, a Canadian economist for NATO, was recruited to the KGB because of his access to top-secret documents. His motivation was not money, but the belief that his spying would help to create world peace. He was arrested while vacationing in London in 1982.

### HANSSEN, ROBERT P.
An FBI counterintelligence officer, Hanssen began spying for the Soviets in 1979. He betrayed details of US security programs and even the location of the underground bunker where the US government would be housed in the event of a nuclear war. His information also led to the execution of three US agents in Russia. In 2001, Hanssen was arrested in Vienna, Virginia, while trying to hide secret FBI documents.

### HERRMANN, RUDOLPH
This KGB mole entered the US from Canada in 1968 and spied while posing as a photographer. He acted as a courier for the KGB, transmitting material collected by other spies. After his arrest by the FBI in 1977, Hermann worked as a double agent until his mission ended in 1980.

### HOWARD, EDWARD L.
In 1983, Howard was forced to resign from the CIA after failing a lie-detector test when quizzed about theft and drug use. Two years later he was revealed as a KGB spy by Soviet defector Vitaly Yurchenko. Howard eluded his FBI surveillance and fled to the Soviet Union.

*Robert P. Hanssen*

### ISMAYLOV, VLADIMIR M.
In 1986, Ismaylov, a Soviet military attaché stationed in Washington, D.C., persuaded a US Air Force officer (really an FBI undercover agent) to supply him with secret military data. He was detained at the drop site in Maryland. Because of his diplomatic status, he could not be tried, so he was expelled from the US.

### KHOKOLOV, NIKOLAI
A Soviet intelligence officer, Khokolov trained as an assassin in 1953. His first target was the Russian leader of an anti-Soviet political party based in West Germany. Khokolov's weapon was a pistol fitted inside a gold cigarette case. Instead of carrying out the job, he defected to the US, where he revealed much about the Soviet murder program. Khokolov himself narrowly survived poisoning by Russian agents in 1957.

### KOECHER, KARL F.
In 1965, Karl Koecher, a Czech mole, and his wife Hana staged a phoney defection to the US, where Koecher later obtained a job with the CIA translating top-secret materials. Until his arrest in 1983, he passed classified information to the KGB and Czech intelligence, including the names of CIA agents. He was exchanged for Soviet dissident Anatoly Shcharansky in 1986.

## LONSDALE, GORDON
om 1955 to 1961, when he was arrested by
5, Lonsdale was the chief Soviet mole in
itain. His real name was Konon Molody, but
posed as a Canadian businessman. Lonsdale
as part of a spy ring that revealed details of
itain's underwater weapons systems. In 1964,
was exchanged for Greville Wynne, a British
ent being held by the Soviets.

## ERCADER, RAMÓN
anish-born Mercader was trained as an
sassin by the Soviet intelligence service. In
40, he was sent to Mexico City to kill Leon
oksky, the exiled opponent of Soviet dictator
sef Stalin. Mercader visited Trotsky's home
ask him to review an article he had written
r a newspaper. While Trotsky read the piece,
ercader hit him in the head with an ice ax
d he died the next day. After 20 years in a
exican prison, Mercader returned to
oscow a hero.

## ICHELSON, ALICE
1984, Michelson, an East German,
as arrested when boarding a
ane from New York to
zechoslovakia with
pe recordings
dden in a
garette pack.
ichelson was
ting as a courier
r Soviet
telligence. Before
r case came to trial,
e was exchanged
ong with three other
ast European spies for 25
eople imprisoned in East
ermany and Poland. It was
e biggest ever "spy swap."

## ONTES, ANA B.
ontes was motivated to spy by
er political beliefs, rather than
oney. She was recruited as a
uban spy in 1984, while still in
ollege. She began work in the US DIA
Defense Intelligence Agency) in 1985, and
ovided top-secret information to the Cuban
telligence service until her arrest in 2001.

## ICHOLSON, HAROLD J.
n his arrest at Dulles International Airport,
ashington, D.C., in 1996, Harold Nicholson
as found to be carrying rolls of film bearing
nages of top-secret documents. Nicholson, the
ighest ranking CIA officer ever
narged with espionage, began
ying for Russian intelligence in
994. For two and a half years he
acked into the CIA's computer
ystem and provided the Russians
ith every secret he could steal.

## ORWOOD, MELITA
he longest-serving Soviet spy in
ritain, Melita Norwood began
ying in 1938. When working as
typist for a company involved
Britain's top-secret project to
evelop an atomic bomb, she
pplied nuclear secrets to the
oviet Union. Norwood was not
evealed as a spy until 1999, when
e was 87. Because of her age,
he British authorities decided not
prosecute her.

*Ana B. Montes*

## PITTS, EARL E.
In return for payments totaling $224,000,
FBI special agent Pitts gave classified
material to first Soviet and then
Russian intelligence services
between 1987 and 1992, including
a list of FBI informants in Russia.
Pitts was unmasked with the help
of his wife Mary, who told another
FBI agent of her suspicions.

## POLLARD, JONATHAN J.
Arrested in 1985, Pollard was a
US naval intelligence analyst and
Israeli spy. He provided so much
top-secret information to his
Israeli handlers that they had to
set up a high-speed "copy shop"
in the home of an Israeli staff
member, using the latest
photocopying machines.

*Jonathan J. Pollard*

## REGAN, BRIAN
In 2001, Regan, a retired
US Air Force sergeant, was
arrested in Washington,
D.C., while attempting
to board a plane
bound for Switzerland. A
ciphered message was discovered inside
his shoe. It took months to decode, but
it finally revealed the locations where
Regan had buried 21 caches of secret
US documents. Regan, who was
heavily in debt, had tried to contact
the Iraqi dictator Saddam
Hussein to demand
$13 million for
information about
US reconnaissance
satellites.

## REILLY, SIDNEY
A Russian-born adventurer
who spied for MI6 during the
Russian Revolution of 1917, Reilly
"Ace of Spies" was a master of
disguise who posed as a member of
the Cheka, the Russian secret
police. Once, fearing arrest, he
tore up secret documents he was
carrying and swallowed them.
Reilly later went to live in New
York, but in 1925 he was
persuaded by the British to
return to Moscow, where he
was caught and executed.

## RITTER, NICHOLAS
In the years before World
War II, Ritter, a German
military intelligence
officer, developed agents
in the US and Britain.
His greatest success came
in 1937, when his agent
Herbert Lang supplied
him with top-secret
plans for the Norden
bomb sight, an aiming
device that allowed
high-altitude aircraft to
drop their bombs with
precision. The plans were
cut up and the pieces
mailed to Germany
inside newspapers.

*Harold J. Nicholson*

## SCRANAGE, SHARON M.
While working for the CIA in Ghana in
1983–84, Scranage revealed the identities
of CIA informants and agents to the Ghanaian
intelligence service. The Ghanaians passed
on the damaging
information
about CIA
intelligence
gathering
activities to
Libya, Cuba, East
Germany, and
other allies of
the Soviet Union.
Scranage came
under suspicion in
1985, when she
failed a routine lie-
detector test on her
return to the US.

## SHADRIN, NIKOLAI
A Soviet naval officer
who defected to the
US, Shadrin (real name
Nikolai Artamanov)
was forced by the FBI
to become a double
agent in 1966. When
Shadrin visited Vienna, Austria, in 1975, he was
abducted by KGB officers and was accidentally
killed in a struggle with his captors.

## TREHOLT, ARNE
The head of the Norwegian Foreign
Ministry's press office, Treholt was
arrested while boarding a flight
from Norway to
Austria with
a suitcase
full of
classified
documents
for the KGB.
A search of his
home revealed
a further 6,000
pages of secret
NATO material.
Treholt had first
come under
suspicion in 1980,
when he was part of
Norway's delegation
to the United Nations.

*Arthur James Walker*

## WALKER, ARTHUR J.
Beginning in 1980,
Walker, a retired US
Navy lieutenant-
commander, passed
information about the
design and construction of US warships to his
brother John (*see* p. 8), a KGB spy, while
working for a defense company in Virginia. The
Walker spy ring, which also included John's son
Michael and Jerry Whitworth (below), was
one of the most damaging in US history.

## WHITWORTH, JERRY ALFRED
A collaborator with the Walkers (above), Jerry
Whitworth gave the Soviets information on US
naval communications between 1975 and 1982.
The "key lists" that he supplied, along with details
of the Navy's cryptographic equipment, enabled
the Soviets to decode US naval messages. John
and Michael Walker testified against Whitworth
in return for a lesser sentence for Michael Walker.

# Timeline of modern spying

THERE HAVE ALWAYS BEEN SPIES, but the early 20th century marked the start of a "golden age" of spying, as powerful nations came head to head in the political arena and on the battlefield. In particular, the Cold War era following World War II saw unprecedented levels of espionage, with the US and the Soviet Union vying for supremacy on the world stage.

**1909**
The British Secret Service Bureau is set up. It will later give rise to MI6, the agency for protecting and promoting British security overseas.

**1917**
Mata Hari is executed in Paris after a trial in which she is used as a scapegoat to blame French military failures on enemy spies.

**1917**
Founding of the Cheka (Russian Security and Intelligence Service) in St. Petersburg. Under the Soviets, the Cheka will later become the KGB.

**1918**
The Soviet Union forms the Chief Intelligence Directorate of the General Staff (GRU) to focus on the collection of military information abroad.

**1923**
German engineer Arthur Scherbius exhibits his Enigma ciphering machine, which Germany will use for secret communication in World War II.

**1929**
In 1929, Henry L. Stimson, the US Secretary of State, closes the US Cipher Bureau, proclaiming "Gentlemen do not read each other's mail."

**1939**
World War II begins, with the invasion of Poland by the forces of Nazi Germany.

**1940**
Leon Trotsky, the exiled opponent of Soviet Union dictator Josef Stalin, is murdered in Mexico, having been tracked by Stalin's spies for 12 years.

**1940**
Britain forms the Special Operations Executive (SOE). Prime Minister Winston Churchill orders its head, Hugh Dalton, to "set Europe ablaze!"

Leon Trotsky lies dying in a hospital bed, 1940

**1941**
The US creates the COI (Coordinator of Information), the world's first centralized intelligence service.

**1941**
Caught unaware, the US suffers a devastating attack by Japanese aircraft on Pearl Harbor and other naval bases in the Hawaiian islands. The attack is a major failure by US intelligence.

A US warship burns in Pearl Harbor, 1941

**1941**
Soviet spy Richard Sorge warns Stalin of German plans to attack Russia, but he is ignored. He also accurately predicts Japan's invasion of the Dutch East Indies to replace its dwindling oil reserves.

**1942**
The US creates the Office of Strategic Services (OSS) to succeed the COI.

**1943**
The British attach mock "secret plans" to a dead body and let it wash up on a Spanish beach. The plans convince the Germans that the Allies are planning to invade the Balkans and Sardinia instead of the island of Sicily, the real target.

**1943**
Russian scientist Lev Sergeivich Theremin converts a light bulb into a listening device by targeting it with a radarlike signal. It can pick up all conversation taking place around it.

**1943**
The Allies meet in Tehran, Iran, to plan the last phase of the war against Germany. The Soviets use bugs to eavesdrop on the US delegation and learn of their secret negotiating positions.

**1944**
The world's first programmable electronic computer, Colossus, is used at Bletchley Park, England, to decipher German communications in advance of the D-Day invasion.

Colossus computer at Bletchley Park, 1944

**1945**
World War II ends in victory for the Allies, but in its aftermath the Cold War begins. The West is separated from the Soviet Union and its Communist allies by the military, political, and ideological barrier known as the Iron Curtain.

**1945**
Captured German Enigma cipher machines are repaired by the British and later presented to other nations for use in secret communications. The countries that receive them are not told that the British can decipher the messages they send.

**1945**
Harry Truman, US vice president, succeeds Theodore Roosevelt as president. Truman learns for the first time of the secret US atomic bomb project. The Soviet leader Josef Stalin already knows of the secret, thanks to his spy networks.

**1947**
President Harry Truman establishes the Central Intelligence Agency (CIA).

**1947**
Soviet intelligence successfully eavesdrops on every foreign embassy in Moscow.

**1949**
The Soviet Union tests its first atomic bomb years ahead of Western expectations, due to the successful theft of atomic secrets from the West.

**1950**
US Senator Joseph McCarthy causes anti-Communist hysteria by alleging that the US government is heavily infiltrated by Communist spies. Decades later Soviet spy archives will reveal that, though exaggerated, the claims are at least partly true.

**1952**
In Moscow, a wooden eagle plaque given to the US Ambassador in 1945 by Russian "Young Pioneers" (boy scouts) is found to be bugged. Every word spoken in the Ambassador's office has been heard by the Soviets for seven years.

**1953**
After an uprising believed to have been stirred up by Western intelligence, East Germany forms its secret police, the Ministry for State Security (Stasi).

**1953**
Julius and Ethel Rosenberg, two American Communists, are executed for passing nuclear weapons secrets to the Soviet Union in wartime.

**1955**
The CIA and MI6 build a spy tunnel under the streets of Soviet-occupied East Berlin to tap into a communication cable between Soviet military forces and Moscow. MI6 officer George Blake, a KGB double agent, gives information that enables the Soviets to "discover" the tunnel in 1956.

**1956**
First flight over the Soviet Union by the new US high-altitude U2 spy plane.

**1959**
The first Corona satellite is launched, one of a series of satellites used by the CIA to photograph the Soviet Union, China, and other areas.

**1960**
A CIA U2 spy plane piloted by Francis Gary Powers is shot down over the Soviet Union.

**1961**
Because of Cuba's close links with the Soviet Union, President John F. Kennedy authorizes an invasion. A CIA-armed and -trained force (the 2506 Brigade) lands at the Bay of Pigs. The Cubans easily fight off the invasion.

**1963**
In the UK it is revealed that John Profumo, Secretary of State for War, has had an affair with the showgirl Christine Keeler, who was also involved with a Russian naval attaché (and GRU intelligence officer).

**1963**
The CIA offers a pen containing a poison-filled hypodermic needle to a Cuban agent to assassinate Cuban leader Fidel Castro. It is never used.

**1963**
Ex-MI6 officer Kim Philby is revealed as a KGB agent. He escapes to the USSR.

**1967**
US naval officer John Walker volunteers as a Soviet spy. During the next 17 years, Walker's information will enable the Soviets to decipher over a million secret messages.

**1972**
Sir Anthony Blunt, former Surveyor of the Queen's Pictures, is revealed as having been a KGB spy from the 1930s to the 1950s. He was one of the "Cambridge Five" (*see* p. 59).

**1974**
A US vessel posing as a deep-sea drilling platform recovers part of K-129, a Soviet submarine that sank in 1968 in 16,800 ft (5,120 m) of water.

**1978**
Aided by the KGB, Bulgarian agents kill Bulgarian dissident Georgi Markov in London, jabbing him with a poison-tipped umbrella.

**1979**
FBI agent Robert Hanssen walks into the Soviet American Trading Organization in New York City and offers to spy for the Soviets.

**1980**
CIA disguise expert Tony Mendez invents a fake Canadian movie project and travels to Iran to check out filming locations. He brings six US hostages out of Iran disguised as part of his film crew.

**1981**
Turkish gunman Ahmet Ali Agca shoots and wounds Pope John Paul II in Rome. Italy accuses the Bulgarian secret service of being behind the shooting.

**1985**
KGB Colonel Oleg Gordievsky, a mole for MI6, escapes from Moscow while under surveillance by the KGB's 7th Directorate.

**1985**
KGB Commander Vitaly Yurchenko defects to the CIA in Rome and is secretly flown to the US. He soon redefects, claiming that he had been kidnapped and drugged by the Americans.

**1985**
CIA officer Aldrich Ames offers to work for the KGB. He reveals all US sources inside the KGB, resulting in at least 10 deaths.

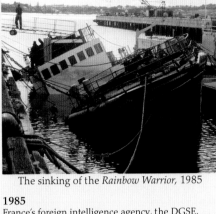

The sinking of the *Rainbow Warrior*, 1985

**1985**
France's foreign intelligence agency, the DGSE, sinks the Greenpeace ship *Rainbow Warrior* in New Zealand, to prevent it from obstructing a French nuclear test in the Pacific Ocean.

**1986**
A defector alerts the CIA to the use of "spy dust" (nitrophenylpentadienal, or NPPD) by the KGB in Moscow to track the movements of suspected CIA and MI6 officers posing as diplomats.

**1986**
Israeli dissident Mordechai Vanunu travels to London with photos of Israel's secret nuclear program. He is lured to Rome by "Cindy," an Israeli agent posing as a US tourist, then drugged, taken back to Israel, and imprisoned.

**1989**
The Berlin Wall, which has divided Berlin since 1962, is torn down.

**1991**
The Soviet Union breaks up, marking the end of the Cold War and the Iron Curtain. The now-defunct KGB's foreign-intelligence activities will be taken over by a new Russian agency, the SVR.

**1992**
Former KGB archivist Vasili Mitrokhin defects to the UK, revealing that he has buried thousands of secret notes under his house near Moscow.

**1999**
FBI agent and SVR mole Robert Hanssen tells the Russians of a secret eavesdropping tunnel under the Russian embassy in Washington, D.C.

**1999**
SVR officer Stanislav Gussef is arrested outside the US State Department in Washington, D.C., where he has secretly bugged a conference room.

**2003**
The US and its allies invade Iraq, saying that it has "weapons of mass destruction." Much of the evidence used to justify the invasion, from Iraqi defector Rafid Ahmed Alwan, turns out to be false.

**2006**
Alexander Litvinenko, former lieutenant-colonel of Russia's Federal Security Service (FSB), dies in London of radiation sickness. Russian agents are suspected of causing his illness.

**2006**
Russia claims that British spies have been sending secret information using a transmitter hidden inside a fake rock on a Moscow street.

The end of the Berlin Wall, 1989

President John F. Kennedy, who authorized a CIA-backed invasion of Cuba in 1961

# Find out more

IN ADDITION TO GATHERING INFORMATION from secret sources, intelligence officers use "open sources," such as newspapers, television news, and internet blogs. Today, the internet is the largest store of open-source information. Many of the tools used by intelligence officers (such as the internet search engine Google™) are available to you on your home computer. So start discovering more about spying by going online. You can learn espionage skills on visits to spy-themed museums, exhibitions, and leisure attractions. Novels and movies can also give an entertaining (if not authentic) flavor of the secret life of spies.

## Spies on film

James Bond (007) is the world's most famous movie spy. Created by writer Ian Fleming in 1953, he was featured in 12 novels, although more than Bond 20 films have been made to date. The movie series began in 1962 with *Dr. No*; recent Bond movies include *Casino Royale* (2006) and *Quantum of Solace* (2008).

Recently, Bond's popularity has been rivaled by a new character, Jason Bourne. The movies *The Bourne Identity* (2002), *The Bourne Supremacy* (2004), and *The Bourne Ultimatum* (2007) were adapted from novels by Robert Ludlum. They feature the escapades of Jason Bourne, a CIA intelligence officer who has lost his memory.

Many purists who understand the real nature of espionage consider the best spy film to be *The Spy Who Came in from the Cold* (1965), based on John le Carré's novel of the same name.

Scene from Austin Powers spy-spoof film

In addition to action heroes, there have been comedy spies, including Austin Powers, who made his debut in *Austin Powers: International Man of Mystery* (1997), and *Johnny English* (2003)—a spoof of James Bond.

Films for children include *Spy Kids* (2001), *Spy Kids 2: Island of Lost Dreams* (2002), and *Spy Kids 3-D: Game Over* (2003). These movies feature the adventures of Juni and Carmen Cortez, children of superspy parents. Alex Rider, the teenage boy forced to join MI6, made the leap from the novel to the big screen in 2006 with the movie *Stormbreaker*.

### INTERNATIONAL SPY MUSEUM
The world's largest public spy museum is located in Washington, D.C. Visitors to the International Spy Museum first learn the skills of espionage and then see how famous (and not so famous) spies have secretly influenced world events. Spy fiction is also covered here: James Bond's Aston Martin DB5 car from the movie *Goldfinger* (1964) is one of the museum's most popular attractions.

### SPY BOOKS
Few spy novels are realistic: espionage is actually about secretly and methodically gathering information useful to your government, rather than thrill-a-minute, explosion-filled adventures. But spy novels can be entertaining nevertheless. Among the spy books for young readers are Charlie Higson's stories about the young James Bond, such as *Double or Die* (2007) and *By Royal Command* (2008), and Anthony Horowitz's tales of the teenage superspy Alex Rider, which include *Stormbreaker* (2000) and *Snakehead* (2007).

Exhibits at the International Spy Museum, Washington, D.C.

## USEFUL WEBSITES

- Discover all about satellites and how they are used for reconnaissance and data collection at the website of the US's National Reconnaissance Office: www.nrojr.gov/
- This cool site allows you to select from a secret mission and "go operational": www.dia.mil/kids/interfacemx.html
- The FBI's Kids' Page shows how FBI special agents and analysts investigate cases, and introduces the CIA's working dogs. There are plenty of games, tips, stories, and interactive activities: www.fbi.gov/fbikids.htm
- America's National Security Agency has a page for CryptoKids, with details on how to make and break codes and ciphers, as well as games and activities, and a reference page for teachers: www.nsa.gov/kids/
- The CIA has an excellent and comprehensive website, complete with pages for young people of different ages, as well as teaching resources: www.cia.gov/kids-page/index.html
- The International Spy Museum has one of the top spy sites on the web: www.spymuseum.org/
- Topspysecrets.com has a wealth of information about spies and spying (both real and fictional), including details on how to make spy equipment: www.topspysecrets.com/index.html
- Check out the website of the National Cryptologic Museum, Maryland: www.nsa.gov/MUSEUM/
- The US Counterintelligence Centre's website has an extensive archive: www.cicentre.com
- The website of the Bletchley Park Museum, UK, has in-depth information about code-breaking in World War II: www.bletchleypark.org.uk/
- The Spy Museum in Tampere, Finland, records the history of espionage. It was the world's first public spy museum. www.vakoilumuseo.fi/englanti/

Cryptanalyst's headphones and message transcripts at Bletchley Park, UK

### BLETCHLEY PARK MUSEUM
In World War II, Bletchley Park, near Milton Keynes in the UK, was the headquarters of British intelligence and the center of its code-breaking activities. Among the exhibits are reconstructions of the Bombe, the machine used to break Germany's Enigma codes, and Colossus, the world's first programmable electronic computer, which cracked the codes of Lorenz, another German cipher machine. The collection also includes cipher machines from the Cold War period.

Enigma machines at the National Cryptologic Museum, Maryland

Examining bugging devices at Spymasters in Cambridge, UK

### NATIONAL CRYPTOLOGIC MUSEUM
Located next to headquarters of the National Security Agency at Fort George G. Meade, Maryland, this museum contains thousands of artifacts that trace the dramatic role cryptology has played in US history. Visitors learn about the people who devoted their lives to cryptology, the machines and devices they developed, the techniques they used, and the places where they worked.

### TEST YOUR SPY SKILLS
There is a growing number of leisure attractions where you can get hands-on experience of spy equipment, acquire some spy skills, and see how you fare as a spy in role-play scenarios. At Spymasters, in Cambridge, UK, visitors undertake missions to steal secrets from a mocked-up foreign embassy, taking care to avoid detection by alarms, sensors, and cameras.

# Glossary

**AGENT** A person who works for, but is not officially employed by, an intelligence service.

**AGENT IN PLACE** An agent recruited by an intelligence service who already works for the target organization.

**AGENCY** An intelligence service or a body responsible for some aspect of national security.

**ASSASSIN** Someone who murders a politically important person, either for money or other rewards or for political reasons.

**BUG** A hidden microphone, often linked to a transmitter, for secretly listening to conversations.

**CCTV** (Closed-Circuit Television) Video cameras used to transmit signals to a specific, limited set of monitors. The signal is not openly broadcast, as in normal television. CCTV is widely used for security surveillance.

**CHEKA** (Russian abbreviation for Extraordinary Commission for the Struggle against Counter-revolution, Espionage, Speculation, and Sabotage) Cheka was the Russian secret police, founded in 1917. It eventually gave rise to the KGB.

**CIA** (Central Intelligence Agency) The US agency responsible for worldwide intelligence gathering and counterintelligence abroad.

**CIPHER** A type of code that cannot be understood without access to a secret "key" for decrypting messages.

Camera concealed in a book

**CONCEALMENT** Hiding messages, ciphers, bugs, or other espionage materials in specially adapted everyday objects.

**COUNTER-ESPIONAGE** Operations to penetrate a hostile foreign intelligence service.

**COUNTERINTELLIGENCE** A broad term that includes actions against foreign intelligence services, and the protection of people, information, equipment, and installations from espionage, sabotage, and terrorism.

**COURIER** A person who carries secret material for an intelligence service, either knowingly or unknowingly.

**CRYPTANALYSIS** Also known as code-breaking, this is the study of ciphers and other kinds of codes to reveal their hidden messages.

**DEAD DROP** A hiding place, usually in a concealed container, used for secret communication and exchange of material between a spy and his or her handler.

**DEFECTOR** A person who, by choice, leaves a country and flees the control of its intelligence service in order to serve the interests of another country.

**DGSE** (*Direction Générale de la Sécurité Extérieure*) France's external intelligence service, similar in function to the US's CIA and Britain's MI6.

**DOUBLE AGENT** An agent of one intelligence service who is recruited and controlled by another intelligence service, and who secretly works against their original service.

**ELINT** (Electronic Intelligence) Information obtained by intercepting machine-to-machine electronic communications, such as by spy aircraft "listening" to enemy radars.

**ENIGMA** An electromechanical cipher machine used by the German military and government for ciphering and deciphering messages in World War II. Cracking the Enigma codes was vital to the Allies' success in World War II.

**ESPIONAGE** Using spies to obtain secret or confidential information about the plans and activities of a foreign government, a competing business, or other organizations.

**FBI** (Federal Bureau of Investigation) The agency responsible for counterintelligence and other law-enforcement duties within the United States.

Cheka identity card

**CODE** A system for conveying messages by systematically substituting letters, numbers, or symbols for the original text of a message.

**COLD WAR** The state of conflict, tension, and competition that existed between the United States and the Soviet Union and their allies between 1945 and 1991.

**COMINT** (Communications Intelligence) Information derived by intercepting communications between people, via phone taps, mail tampering, and room bugs.

**FLAPS AND SEALS** A term for opening, examining, and resealing envelopes and packages without raising the suspicion of the recipient.

**GESTAPO** (Abbreviation of *Geheime Staatspolizei*) Founded by the Nazi Party, the Gestapo was Germany's secret police in World War II, responsible for internal security.

**GRU** (Russian abbreviation for Chief Intelligence Directorate) Founded in 1918 as the Russian military intelligence service, the GRU survived the fall of the Soviet Union in 1991 and has continued serving the state of Russia.

**HANDLER** An intelligence officer who is responsible for, or controls, an agent.

**HUMINT** (Human Intelligence) Information directly collected by agents themselves, as opposed to information collected by equipment and technology.

Briefcase containing a concealed flaps and seals kit, 1960s

**HYDROPHONE** A device designed to be used underwater for recording or listening to sound.

**ILLEGAL** An agent operating in a foreign country without diplomatic protection, but with a false identity. An illegal usually has no contact with his or her own embassy and is controlled by intelligence services in their own country.

**IMINT** (Image Intelligence) Intelligence in the form of images gathered by cameras and radar on spy aircraft and satellites.

**INDUSTRIAL ESPIONAGE** The secret acquisition of information about business. It may be carried out by a competing firm or by an intelligence officer.

Badge of the United States' NSA

**INFORMER** Someone who reveals secret or confidential information, often for money.

**INTELLIGENCE** The profession of espionage, the information collected by espionage, or the final analyzed product.

**IRON CURTAIN** The military, political, and ideological barrier that existed between the countries of the West and the Soviet Union and its Communist allies from 1945 to 1991.

**KGB** (Russian abbreviation for Committee for State Security) The KGB was the intelligence and security agency in the Soviet Union from 1954 to 1991.

**LISTENING POST (LP)** A site at which signals received by bugs and other means of electronic audio surveillance are monitored.

**MI5** (Military Intelligence, section 5) Britain's MI5 no longer has military connections. Officially called the Secret Service, it is responsible for internal security (within the UK).

**MI6** (Military Intelligence, section 6) Britain's MI6 is no longer associated with the military and is responsible for foreign intelligence. It is officially called the Secret Intelligence Service (SIS).

**MICRODOT** An optical reduction of a text, images, or a photographic negative to a size (usually 1 mm across or smaller) that is illegible without magnification.

**MOLE** An employee or officer of an intelligence service who works secretly for another intelligence service.

KGB badge

**MORSE CODE** An internationally recognized code that substitutes sequences of dots and dashes for letters and numbers.

**MOSSAD** (Hebrew abbreviation for Institute for Intelligence and Special Operations). Mossad is Israel's foreign-intelligence gathering agency.

**NATO** (North Atlantic Treaty Organization) A military alliance, originally established during the Cold War, made up of countries from North America and Western Europe.

**NEUTRALIZE** To render a spy ineffective, such as by exposing them publicly so they cannot work secretly, expelling them to their home country, or prosecuting and imprisoning them.

**NSA** (National Security Agency) The US agency responsible for protecting government information and communications, often by encryption. It also collects and analyzes foreign signals, often by cryptanalysis.

**OPERATIVE** An officer or agent operating under the control of an intelligence service.

**PICKLOCKS** Specially shaped tools that enable the user to unlock doors without a key.

**PLANT** A spy who works his or her way into a target organization in order to collect intelligence.

**RECEIVER** An electronic device that receives signals from a transmitter.

**RECONNAISSANCE** A mission undertaken to secure information, usually in advance of a secret operation.

**RFID CHIP** (Radio-Frequency Identification chip) A tiny computer chip that transmits radio signals. RFID chips can be embedded in passports and ID cards to prevent identity fraud. They are also used on some supermarket goods to monitor purchases, and as secret "tags" by some security services to track the movements of known spies.

**SABOTAGE** Covert actions that weaken an enemy or opponent through the destruction of property or the disruption of essential services.

**SCRAMBLER** A device that prevents telephone tappers from understanding a conversation, often by rearranging the words spoken.

**SIGINT** (Signals Intelligence) A broad term that refers to intelligence obtained by intercepting enemy signals. It includes COMINT and ELINT.

**SPY** An agent used by a state to obtain secret information about enemies, or someone employed by a business to obtain confidential information about its competitors.

**STASI** (*Staatsicherheitsdienst*) East Germany's state security organization, with a section (the HVA) for conducting foreign intelligence operations. It was dissolved in 1990.

**SURVEILLANCE** Observation from a distance using electronic devices and other equipment, both audio and visual.

**SVR** (Russian abbreviation for Russian Foreign Intelligence Service) The agency that replaced the KGB's foreign intelligence-gathering section, which was disbanded in 1991.

**SWEEP** To check a room for bugs, often with an electronic device known as a "broom."

**TELEPHONE TAPPING** Also called wire tapping, telephone tapping is the monitoring of phone conversations by a third party, often by covert means.

**TERRORISM** Using violent acts, such as bombings, to create widespread fear among opponents in order to achieve a political goal.

**TRANSMITTER** An electronic device that generates electrical, radio, or microwave signals and sends them to a receiver.

**TREASON** A crime that involves a serious act of disloyalty to one's own nation.

**TURN** To force a spy to work against his or her original intelligence service as a double agent, usually by confronting them with evidence of their guilt and offering immunity from prosecution in exchange for cooperation.

**UAV** (Unmanned Aerial Vehicle) An unpiloted aircraft that is remotely controlled or directed by a preprogrammed onboard computer. UAVs are often used for military reconnaissance and attack missions, and also for espionage.

**WALK-IN SPY** A spy who walks in to a foreign embassy and offers to supply secrets.

**WARSAW PACT** The military alliance of the Soviet Union and other Communist countries in Central and Eastern Europe. It existed between 1955 and 1991, during the Cold War.

American radio transmitter and receiver used in World War II

# Index

## A

Abel, Rudolph 39, 62
aerial reconnaissance 20, 38, 39, 52–53
Agca, Ali 65
Agee, Phillip 62
aircraft 18, 52–53
Akbar 40
Alexander the Great 7
Alwan, Rafid Ahmed 65
Ames, Aldrich and Rosario 34 , 65
André, Major John 30
Angleton, James Jesus 50
animal spies 18–21
Ankhesenamen 6
Arnold, Benedict 30
assassinations 36, 43, 68

## B

Babington, Anthony 25
Baden-Powell, Robert 24
Barnett, David H 62
Bayeux Tapestry 6–7
Bell, William H 62
Berlin Wall 38–39, 65
Bible 6
binoculars 13
biometric data 57
birds 18–19, 20
*Blackbird* (spy plane) 52–53
blackmail 8, 12, 40
Blake, George 62, 65
Bletchley Park 26, 67
Blunt, Anthony 59, 65
Boer War 31
Bombe 26, 67
Bond, James 7, 10, 47, 58, 60–61, 66
Bossard, Frank 50
Boyce, Christopher J 62
Boyd, Belle 30
Brandt, Willy 41
briefcases 16–17, 33
bugs 10, 14–17, 20, 44, 45, 48–49, 68
Bull, Gerald 9
Burgess, Guy 35, 59

## C

Caesar, Julius 18
"Cambridge Five" 59, 65
cameras 10–13, 20, 23, 28, 45, 51, 56, 68
Carney, Jeffrey M. 62
cars 46–47
cartoons 31, 48
Castro, Fidel 36, 43, 65
CCTV cameras 45, 51, 56, 68
cell phones 15, 22, 57
Cheka 29, 64, 68
Chin, Larry Wu Tai 9
Churchill, Winston 64
CIA 9, 14, 20–21, 34, 36, 41, 42–43, 50, 53, 60, 64, 65, 68
"Cicero" 31
ciphers 23, 24–25, 26–27, 68
Civil War 30–31
clothing 16, 33, 47
code-breakers 26–27
codes 24–25, 68
Cohen, Eli 62
COI (Coordinator of Information) 64
Cold War 21, 36, 38–39, 40, 48, 53, 54, 59, 64, 65, 68
Coleridge, Major H F 30–31
Colossus 26, 64, 67
COMINT 52, 68
computers 26, 44, 45, 47, 49, 51
concealment 28–29, 68
Conrad, Clyde L 62
Cooper, James Fenimore 60
Cormeau, Yvonne 24, 32–33, 58
counterespionage 50–51, 68
counterintelligence 44, 48–49, 50–51, 68
couriers 22, 68
cover stories 32–33
criminals 55
Cromwell, Thomas 40
cryptanalysts 26–27, 68
crystal radios 32

## D, E

Dalton, Hugh 64
*Darkstar* (UAV) 52, 53
"dead drops" 28, 68
"dead soldier" 27, 64
defectors 34, 50, 68
Deighton, Len 60
Dejean, Maurice 8
DGSE 43, 65, 68
diplomats 9
disguise 28–29, 30
double agents 34–35, 48, 68
dragonflies, robotic 20, 21
drugs, illegal 54
Dukes, Paul 29
Dulles, Allen 60
Dumas, Alexander 60
ELINT 52, 68
Elizabeth I, Queen 28, 41
emails 44
embassies 9
Enigma 25, 26, 64, 67, 68
Eon, Chevalier d' 28, 29
equipment 10–11
espionage 6, 68
execution 30, 39, 50

## F

FBI 40, 41, 45, 47, 55, 65, 68
films 60–61, 66
flaps and seals 50, 68
Fleming, Ian 7, 10, 58, 60–61, 66
Forsyth, Frederick 60
Fraser-Smith, Charles 10, 61
Frederick the Great, King 30
Friedman, William F 27

## G

gadgets 10, 61
General Electric 47
General Motors (GM) 46
Genghis Khan 7
Gestapo 58, 68
Gifford, Gilbert 28
Gimpel, Eric 62
glove pistol 37
Gordievsky, Oleg 35, 65
Gouzenko, Igor 35
GPS 15, 57
GRU 64, 65, 68

guns 36, 37
Gussef, Stanislav 65
Guzman, Abimael 55

## H

Hambleton, Hugh 62
handlers 68
Hanssen, Robert P. 62, 65
Hari, Mata 58, 64
Hastings, Battle of (1066) 6–7
Hayashi, Kenji 47
Henry VIII, King 40
Herrmann, Rudolph 62
Hitachi 47
Hoover, J. Edgar 40, 41
Howard, Edward L. 62
HUMINT 52, 68
hydrophones 54, 68

## I

IBM 47
illegals 68
industrial espionage 44–47, 68
infinity receivers 45
informers 69
infrared light 12, 13
Inglefield, Sir Frederick 20
ink, invisible 22
Insectothopter 21
intelligence 6, 69
International Spy Museum 66
internet 22, 44, 48, 56, 57, 66
iris scanning 57
Iron Curtain 64, 65, 69
Ismaylov, Vladimir M 62
Ivan IV, Czar 40

## J

Jericho 6
John Paul II, Pope 65
Joshua 6
Justinian I, Emperor 46

## K

Keeler, Christine 65
Kennedy, John F. 65
KGB 11, 14, 35, 43, 59, 60, 61, 64, 65, 69
Khokolov, Nikolai 62

70

# Acknowledgments

**Dorling Kindersley would like to thank:**
Audiotel International Limited (Keith Penny, Ray Summers, Julie Walker, Adrian Hickey); Eon Productions (Julie O'Reilly); the Imperial War Museum, London (Paul Cornish, John Bullen, Mike Hibbard); Intelligence Corps Museum, Ashford (Major R W M Shaw, Mrs. Janet Carpenter); Leica UK Ltd. (Peter Mulder); Lorraine Electronics Surveillance (David Benn, Simon Rosser); H Keith Melton; Next Retail Ltd. (Shirley Brown, Hilary Santell); Joanne Poynor; Spycatcher (Mike Phillips); Whitbread plc (Nicholas Redman, Archivist) **Design help:** Ann Cannings, Jason Gonsalves, Sailesh Patel **Pigeon:** Rick Osman; **Pigeon parachute:** Martine Cooper; **Artwork:** John Woodcock; **Endpapers:** Iain Morris; **Index:** Marion Dent

For this edition, the publisher would also like to thank: Lisa Stock for editorial assistance; David Ekholm-JAlbum, Sunita Gahir, Susan St Louis, Lisa Stock, and Bulent Yusuf for the clip art; Sue Nicholson and Edward Kinsey for the wall chart; Hilary Bird for the new index; Stewart J Wild for proofreading; Margaret Parrish and John Searcy for Americanization.

**Picture credits:**

The publisher would like to thank the following for their kind permission to reproduce their photographs:

(Key: a-above; b-below/bottom; c-center; f-far; l-left; r-right; t-top)

**akg-images:** J V Leffdoel *Scipio Publius Cornelius* 40tl; Ullstein Bild 20bl.
**Alamy Images:** Ruth Grimes 17clb (voice recorder in briefcase); Jeff Morgan Technology 58br; Katharine Andriotis Photography, LLC 64-65 (background), 66-67 (background), 68-69 (background), 70-71 (background); Kolvenbach 57tl; Stocksearch 51br; Andrew Twort 10clb; Andrew H. Williams 58l.
**Ancient Art & Architecture Collection:** 6tl, 6bl, 6bc.
**Courtesy of Apple. Apple and the Apple logo are trademarks of Apple Computer Inc., registered in the US and other countries:** 15br.
**Associated Press Ltd.:** 9tr, 29bl, 35t, 35br, 43c, 47bl, 52tr; Wire Photo 53cr.

**Aviation Photographs International:** 38tl.
**Bildarchiv Preussischer Kulturbesitz:** 25cl.
**Bilderdienst Süddeutscher Verlag:** 27cl.
**Bridgeman Art Library:** Guildhall Art Gallery, Corporation of London, Sir John Gilbert, detail from *Ego Et Rex Meus* 40cl; Private Collection, I Glasunov *Ivan The Terrible* 1989, 40bl; by courtesy of the board of Trustees of the V & A, London, Nicholas Hilliard, *Mary Queen of Scots* 28cl.
**Camera Press Ltd.:** 35tr, 39cl; R. Artacho 55cra; S. Ferguson 42br; B. Ross 58ra.
**Jean-Loup Charmet:** Bibliothèque des arts décoratifs, Lucien Laforge *L'Espion*, 1916, 31tc.
**Corbis:** Bettmann 67c; Hulton-Deutsch Collection 66b.
**DC Comics Inc.:** *Spy vs Spy* is a trademark of E.C. Publications, Inc. ©1995. All rights reserved. Used with permission 42t.
**Diasonic:** 17tr.
**DK Images:** H Keith Melton Collection 70b, 70c, 70t, 71b, 71c.
**Eon Productions:** Keith Hamshere / United Artists (*Golden Eye*) front cover bcl, 4cb, 61tr, 61cr, 61br.
**Satellite image courtesy of GeoEye. Copyright 2008. All rights reserved.:** 54tl.
**E.T. Archive:** Biblioteca Nazionale Marciana, Venice 9tr; Musée de Versailles, Philippe de Champaigne, detail from *Cardinal Richelieu* 41cr; Staatliche Glyptothek, Munich 9tl; V & A, London 9tc.
**Frank Spooner Pictures:** Gamma-Liaison 9cl.
**Getty Images:** 66c; AFP 67t; Stuart Paton / The Image Bank 45b; Tom Stoddart Archive 67b.
**Courtesy of Giggle Bug:** 59tr.
**Michael Holford:** Musée de Bayeux / V&A, London: 8-9b.
**Hulton Deutsch Collection:** 8cr, 38c, 41c, 41bl, 58l, 57tc, 59br, 59l.
**Imperial War Museum, London:** 18cr, 23bc, 29tl, 36tr, 58br; Fougasse *Careless Talk Costs Lives* 8tr.
**Courtesy of the International Spy Museum:** © The House on F Street, LLC 2008. All Rights Reserved 68br; © The House on F Street, LLC 2008. All Rights Reserved. 20tl.
**iStockphoto.com:** 12 (camera with zoom lens); Mark Evans 55b.
**The Kobal Collection:** New Line 68bl.
**Lockheed Martin Skunk Works®:** 52-53b, 53t.
**Magnum Photos Ltd.:** E Erwitt 43cl; S Meiselas 54bl; E Reed 17cr; Zachmann 55ca.

**The Mansell Collection:** 8tl.
**Mary Evans Picture Library:** front flap tl, 29r, 40c; J Mammen back cover tr, 12tl.
**H Keith Melton:** front cover br and bcr, back cover rcb, 10br, 11tl, 11tc, 11b,15br, 20cb, 23c, 27cr, 28tl, 28br, 28bl, 28tr, 30br, 36br, 37tr, 37tl, 37c, 37b, 42bl, 43tl, 43tr, 43br, 45tl, 50l, 50-51b, 51cl, 64b, 64c, 64t, 65b, 65ca, 65cb, 65t; Jerry Richards of the FBI Laboratory, Washington DC 8cl, 8c; Jack Ingram, Curator of the National Cryptologic Museum, Maryland 14cl, 14c, 27tr.
**Mirror Syndication International:** 27b, 50tr; Aldus Archive 24tl; Aldus Archive / Science Museum / Eileen Tweedy front cover cr, 24cl; Rijksinstituut voor Oorlogsdocumentatie 9c; National Archives, USA 26c; Public Record Office 25tl, 41 tl; © US Army 27tl.
**NASA:** Paul Riedel / Glenn Research Center (GRC) 5tr.
**National Cryptologic Museum, Maryland:** 26bl, 69c.
**National Portrait Gallery, London:** John De Critz, the Elder *Sir Francis Walsingham* 41 tr.
**Nokia:** 15bl, 16cra (mobile phone).
**PA Photos:** Brien Aho / AP 21tr; Cameron Davidson / AP 21bl; Betsy Gagne / AP 21br; Peter Jordan 69t; Metropolitan Police 58tr; Eckehard Schulz / AP 21tl.
**Peter Newark's American Pictures:** 30tl, 30bc, 31bl.
**Photolibrary:** 44 (main).
**Popperfoto:** 23tl, 31tr, 31br, 35bl, 41 br, 58cl; Reuter / S Jaffe 34br; Reuter / W McNamee 34c.
**Press Association:** 36bcl.
**Range:** Bettmann / UPI 22bl, 50c, 54br; Bettmann / UPI / Sam Schulman 50bc.
**Rex Features Ltd.:** 7br; Action Press 38-39; Sipa-Press 39tl.
**Reuters Television:** front cover tl, 42cr (detail).
**Ronald Grant Archive:** *Stakeout* 1987, Touchstone 14bl, *Doctor No* 1962, UA / Eon 58tr, *The Ipcress File* 1965, Rank / Steven Lowndes 58tr, *The Three Musketeers* 1948, MGM 58br, *The Conversation* 1974, Paramount / Francis Ford Coppola 61bl.
**Science Photo Library:** Andrew Brookes / National Physical Laboratory 59cr; NRSC Ltd. 52c; R. Ressmeyer, Starlight 38bc.
**Science & Society Picture Library, Science Museum, London:** 26tl, 66t.
**Shutterstock:** 57bl; Andrjuss 45c.
**Spy Games Ltd., www.spy-games.com:** 69b.
**Topham-Picturepoint Ltd.:** back cover br, 10tl, 35cla, 35c, 34tl, 34tr; AP 45tc.

**Werner Forman Archive:** Ninja Museum Ueno, detail showing Ninja making secret signs 40bl; E Strouhal 6bl.
**Jo Walton:** 68t.
**Worldmap-Priroda:** 52tl, 52bl.

**Wall chart**
**Alamy Images:** Andrew Twort cra; **The Art Archive:** Science Museum, London / Eileen Tweedy bl; **DK Images:** H Keith Melton Collection clb, tr; RAF Museum, Hendon cl (playing card); Spycatcher cr (street scenes); **iStockphoto.com:** Philippe Devanne cr (SLR camera); **The Kobal Collection:** Danjaq / Eon / UA c; **H. K. Melton:** cl (spy rocks); **NASA:** Paul Riedel / Glenn Research Center (GRC) br.

All other images © Dorling Kindersley For further information see: **www.dkimages.com**